Praise for *If You Feel Too Much*

"Jamie loves people unlike anyone I've ever met. He is also a humble guy and a faithful friend. He's the one who has offered to come on my darkest day, to cry with me, and on my best day to celebrate. His brand of love is one without judgment, boundaries or pretense. This book gives you a wonderful glimpse at Jamie's beautiful heart. You're in for a treat." —BOB GOFF, *New York Times*–bestselling author of *Love Does*

"Jamie is special. He is sincere and sensitive and kind. He has poured his heart into this book, and that's how he lives his life. I hope the honesty in Jamie's story and experiences will help you to be honest in yours." —KYLE KORVER, NBA All-Star

"Through poignant self-reflection and stories that pulse with a poetic rawness, Jamie invites us to be part of a bigger conversation. It's one that leads to community, connection, healing and incredible hope." —DR. GEORGINA SMITH, clinical psychologist

"With this book, you have Jamie's heart in your hands. By honestly sharing his life, in joy and pain, he is teaching others how to do the same. *If You Feel Too Much* is Jamie's guide to loving better and finding joy in being known." —JASON RUSSELL, co-founder of Invisible Children

"It's impossible not to feel it deep in your guts when Jamie writes or speaks. His vivid honesty about the human condition always leaves me simultaneously inspired and feeling less alone. This book can only be summed up by using Jamie's own words—it truly is 'a living, breathing, screaming invitation to believe in better things.'" —KELTIE KNIGHT, TV personality

"There are people that say they care for others. And then there are those that do care. Then there is Jamie, who breathes love. This book is proof."

—Propaganda, hip-hop artist and spoken word poet

"When I first met Jamie, he struck me as someone on a mission. Through his sheer determination, he brought some difficult issues out of the shadows and helped so many people realize they were not alone. I believe this book will inspire others to do the same, to get help, and to chase their passion just as he has."

—Kevin Lyman, founder and producer of the Vans Warped Tour

IF YOU FEEL TOO MUCH

IF YOU FEEL TOO MUCH

Thoughts on Things Found and Lost and Hoped For

JAMIE TWORKOWSKI

A TarcherPerigee Book

tarcherperigee

An imprint of Penguin Random House LLC
375 Hudson Street
New York, New York 10014

First hardcover edition 2015
This edition published 2016

Most TarcherPerigee books are available at special quantity discounts for bulk purchase for sales promotions, premiums, fund-raising, and educational needs. Special books or book excerpts also can be created to fit specific needs. For details, write: SpecialMarkets@penguinrandomhouse.com.

Library of Congress Cataloging-in-Publication Data

Tworkowski, Jamie.
If you feel too much : thoughts on things found and lost and hoped for / Jamie Tworkowski ; foreword by Donald Miller.
p.   cm.
Includes bibliographical references.
ISBN 978-0-399-17649-4 (hardback)
1. Tworkowski, Jamie.   2. Conduct of life.   3. Life—Philosophy.   I. Title.
BJ1589.T96   2015   2015010647
170'.44—dc23

ISBN 978-1-101-98272-3

Printed in the United States of America
10 9 8 7 6 5 4 3 2 1

BOOK DESIGN BY NICOLE LAROCHE

*This book is dedicated to my parents, Joe and Janet, and
to my sisters, Jessica and Emily.*

MOM: Your love is a miracle in my life. Thank you for
your constant encouragement. i hope this makes you
proud.

DAD: You gave me surfing and music. You taught me
road trips and t-shirts and even words as well. i wrote
this on your shoulders.

JESS: You're an anchor and a gift to so many. You are
extraordinary when it comes to loving people. Thanks
for all you have refused to give up on, including me.

EM: You are mystery and laughter, but beyond all that,
you have a heart that sees so many things. i promise to
let you name the next book.

AND TO DAVID KUO, WHO DIED BUT ALSO LIVED: What a
joy it was to know you, and to be known by you.
Thanks for what you saw in me. And thanks for giving
me a glimpse.

CONTENTS

THE NEW YORK YEARS (2009–2011)

MILLION-DOLLAR DAYS (2011–2012)

Oscar Wilde said that art reveals more about the one who interprets the art than the artist herself. This may be true in the following memory of Jamie Tworkowski, a man who was particularly struck by a metal bird carrying the mantra "Travel lightly and deeply." The bird is on a wall in our guest room. Few have paid those words any attention but Jamie; few live them out as he does.

Jamie, you are a deep river. You feel every bend and rock deeply. And yet, you are still floating through, still searching and looking. Still traveling light and deeply on a pilgrimage toward a hope that you have never seen. I'm honored to walk beside you, bro. Thank you for your friendship. And until your river finds the sea . . . the bird room is yours whenever you need it.

—Jon Foreman

IF YOU FEEL TOO MUCH

AUTHOR'S NOTE

March 3, 2016
Melbourne Beach, Florida

My hope was that this collection of stories could have a home, a place to be found and shared, and that, for those who ended up with the book in their hands, the stories might provide a sense of home as well. Home meaning you belong, you feel safe, you're not alone. And of course the goal was also hope, that people would be encouraged by the words.

May 26, 2015 was the big day, and it was something like a dream, a very busy dream. My first book release, hours of interviews before a live webcast from the publisher's office, all of it leading up to the book tour's opening night in New York City, friends and family in the crowd. It was a day i won't forget, and things did not slow down from there.

From New York, the tour headed west to Los Angeles, and to eighteen cities after that. i got to share my stories all across America, from Seattle to my hometown of Melbourne, Florida, with Boston and Houston and Chicago in between. There was one night in Toronto, and the tour made it all the way to Honolulu. (Hawaii is perfect. Perfect places have bookstores.)

The days were full of early flights and late night drives to the next city, chasing chances to talk about my book on local news and local radio. Every single event was such a joy, with folks often coming from hours away. For me it was a great privilege to share the stories of my life, to read the pages i had written. i met more than two thousand people on the book tour, and so many of them shared their stories with me, why they had come to the event, what TWLOHA had meant to them, the things that made it personal. These were people who could relate to the experience of pain and the need for hope. There were autographs and pictures but the brief honest exchanges are what stayed with me and kept me going.

It was a day off in Nashville and i was having lunch with my best friend Mark when my phone rang. i need to be honest here and tell you that we were at Chili's. Nashville has plenty of great restaurants and so we took some heat for this, but there was a Chili's two blocks from our hotel, and well, we love Chili's. So anyway, we're sitting there enjoying chips and queso when my phone rings. The call is from a New York phone number and it's one i don't have saved. As an introvert, i hardly answer calls from numbers i *do* have saved, so voicemail seemed a solid option. But the New York area code was enough to make me curious.

"Hello."

It was Sara and Brianna from the publisher. Sara is my editor and Brianna handled publicity and marketing for this book. We had traded emails nearly every day but it was rare for them to call, especially out of the blue. And why were they both on the phone?

"Congratulations! We're calling to let you know that you're a *New York Times* bestselling author."

Mark somehow sensed this was a big moment, so there's actually a video of the phone call. If you were to see this video, you would see me speechless, mouth wide open, then smiling and eventually saying "What?? Noooo waaaay."

The next day we were at Parnassus Books in Nashville. The place was completely packed, with people standing and sitting all around the store, another fifty forced to watch from just outside. Some of my favorite friends were in the room. Renee Yohe was there. She's the one who inspired the "To Write Love on Her Arms" story back in 2006. Matt Wertz sang a song called "To Be Free," and Steven McMorran sang "Ring the Bells," a song you'll hear more about in the pages ahead. After the event, we ended up at Donald Miller's house. Don is my friend but he's also my favorite writer, and very much a hero of mine. i had been talking to Don about a book for years and the dream had finally come true. To celebrate with him and to hear that he was proud of me, of course it meant a lot.

Melbourne, Florida was by far the smallest city on the book

tour, and i wondered if it might have been a bad idea. The thought of my parents and TWLOHA staff and a hundred empty chairs—well that would not be good. Instead, the hometown stop turned out to be the biggest of the tour. My nephew Landon, three at the time, stole the show with his announcement, "Ladies and gentlemen, welcome to Uncle Jamie's book party!" From my spot at the podium, i could see the smiles of former teachers, childhood friends, and yes my mom and dad. The town had filled the chairs.

Nearly a year has passed since *If You Feel Too Much* was first released. i still see tweets and photos nearly every single day—people sitting with the stories, finding encouragement in the words, finding hope and sharing what they find. There are stories of people buying ten copies for their friends, people reading the book again and again, some going to sleep listening to the audio version, to feel a little less alone.

Just today, a few minutes ago, there was an email from my editor Sara. She wrote with the good news that *If You Feel Too Much* is being translated into Polish. (You may have noticed my last name. My great grandparents came from Poland in 1907. What an honor to think that my book is headed back there.)

The whole process has been more than anything i could have imagined. These stories are no longer only mine. Yes i lived and wrote them, but they have taken on lives of their own, colliding with the experiences of so many individuals. It seems there are thousands of us, people navigating fears and dreams, standing at the intersection of pain and hope, wondering if it might be okay to say it all out loud, okay to ask for help.

And on that note, it feels important to be honest. i'm proud and honored and grateful for the journey this book has taken me on. Everything you've read so far is true, but this is true as well: i've been struggling. i've been feeling too much. i've been feeling very sad.

As i write this, it's early March and i am home in Florida. 2016 started off with so much hope. When the ball dropped and millions welcomed midnight, i was falling in love. It was new but it was strong and moving fast, and i've never been more excited, never enjoyed getting to know a person more. Our conversations lasted hours and they began to feel like home. My biggest dream seemed to be coming true: Best friend. The search is over. We started making plans.

The relationship ended recently, on Valentine's Day of all days.

i've cried more in the last three weeks than in the last three years. i am a person who struggles with depression, and seasons of heartache have always been the hardest. This sort of pain shows up in my book but i had been away from it for years. Lately i find myself in a place that is unfortunately familiar.

This book holds stories from a decade of my life. In some

ways, the journey has come full circle. One of the central themes in the pages ahead is the idea that people need other people, that we aren't meant to walk through life alone. i've been reminded of this lately. i am a person in need, and right now i'm leaning on friends and family, asking for advice, asking for perspective. Sometimes i just need someone to listen. Sometimes it's simply not to be alone. It's been a hard road lately, but it would be infinitely harder without the people who love me. This new edition of *If You Feel Too Much* includes five new stories, the final four of which were written in recent days.

Here's my point in sharing all of this:

The things i hope you find inside this book, i'm looking for them too.

i went to counseling yesterday. i'll be back next week, and the week after that.

If you're living with enormous questions, i know the feeling.

If you're struggling, i can say the same.

If you feel too much, i am right there once again.

Life is full of contrast. It's the phone call that your book is a bestseller, and it's the silence when you are asked to unknow your favorite person. It's falling in love and losing love as well. Life is the beauty of your memories and the pain you feel when you remember. There are so many different days.

i still dream of love and hope and home. i ache for peace as i keep searching. i am encouraged by the following: There have

been so many surprises over the years, so many bright moments. When i look back, so much of my life is beyond what i
can explain, beyond what i deserve. i have to keep going, have
to see what's around this corner. i want to know what's at the
end of the road, and the beauty on the way. i want to see the
view the day the fog lifts.

i'm not giving up. The stories you're about to read remind
me not to.

FOREWORD
BY DONALD MILLER

My friend Jamie stayed with Betsy and me last night in Nashville. He stayed for two nights, actually. Jamie runs an organization called To Write Love on Her Arms. It's a voice for the marginalized.

I remember staying up late to hear Jamie speak at a rock concert one night. The band asked him to say something before they went on, and Jamie got up in a sweaty, dark room filled with teenagers. He told them there was much to live for, there were songs and dreams and hopes yet to be created. He reminded them that each of them had come to the concert with somebody else, they'd likely come with a friend, and together they could cling to a hope that in the toughest time, they would be there for each other.

Honestly, I didn't know what to make of it. I wasn't sure whether he was going to pass out flowers or what he was going to do. He just left it at that and walked off the stage.

The kids gathered around him, asking for his autograph, and he uncomfortably signed their shirts and posters.

It's been ten years since I met Jamie. Since then, the organization he started has exploded. He's won awards and grants and appeared on every television show you can think of. People love him. And I swear the guy hasn't changed. He just keeps saying the same thing, softly, as though from some other planet: We need one another. There's no reason to judge. People are more fragile than you could possibly imagine.

I now consider Jamie one of my closest friends. He's the one to call me when I say something unkind online. He reminds me people are hurting and we are supposed to be bigger than the Darwinian games that tempt us. And not only does he call me on my crap, but I call him when I'm hurting.

Anyway, we were sitting out on the back deck and it was cold. Betsy was in the house getting ready for bed. Our dog, Lucy, was chasing a tennis ball that Jamie and I took turns throwing into the yard.

Jamie is a mystery to me, I remember thinking. He doesn't so much tell a story as he is a story. He pours his heart into blogs and he shares them with the world.

Sometimes, though, Jamie wonders whether what he's doing is worth it. Can things as immeasurable as love, acceptance, grace, tolerance, and forgiveness create a better world? These aren't commodities measured in financial exchanges, after all.

Then, sitting there throwing a tennis ball, it occurred to me that Jamie's power is himself. With no fear, he charges his heart at the pointed world as a measure of sacrifice. It has certainly been broken many times. He risks himself by saying how he really feels and standing up to the forces of conformity, most of them dark.

Since meeting Jamie, I've heard countless stories from people who were hurting, lonely, confused, and even suicidal—they were able to find a toehold in his words. They love him because he accepted them as they were, told them they didn't have to act, and let them know their story contributed to the beauty.

I know you and I may not be wired like Jamie, but you are wired like you and I am wired like me. The more fully we live into ourselves, the more impact we will have. Acting may get us the applause we want, but taking a risk on being ourselves is the only path toward true intimacy. And true intimacy, the exchange of affection between two people who are not lying, is transforming.

I wrote Jamie a note the morning he left. I sat in the kitchen with the house still asleep, knowing I'd be gone before he woke up. I sat at the counter and wondered what to say to my friend. How do you tell somebody that without him, the world would be a darker place? So I prayed and asked for a line.

I wrote it down and stuck it in one of the shoes he had left by the front door. It's a true line. It's true of Jamie. But I want it to be true of you too. And for that matter, me. I don't believe we are accidents in the world, and I don't believe we were supposed to be actors either. I think we were supposed to be ourselves and we were meant as a miracle.

Jamie,

Be encouraged. Your heart is writing a poem on the world and it's being turned into a thousand songs.

Much love,
Don

INTRODUCTION

My life changed with a story that i wrote in 2006. i was working as a sales rep for a clothing brand at the time. A job in the surf industry had been my dream since i was a kid. If Hurley's decision to hire me at 22 surprised people, i suppose it was equally surprising when i quit at 26 to start a non-profit. It was an uncertain move for sure, but beyond the uncertainty, a big part of me was simply excited to have the time to write. Writing a book was something i began to dream about and talk about. Publishers and agents reached out. People pitched ideas, fine ideas, but they were books that i did not feel called to write.

i took a sabbatical in the summer of 2013. i was given four months off and decided to spend that time in Los Angeles. My time off taught me that it's one thing to say you're writing a book—that sounds very sexy—but it's another thing entirely to actually write one. As a side note, Los Angeles is a very strange place to take a break. The assumption was that i would write a memoir. Donald Miller's *Blue Like Jazz* was a book that changed a lot of things for me. That book was Don writing about friendships and questions and crushes. The writing was honest and poetic and i loved the freedom of it, the way this one book could tell so many different stories. My journey, especially in recent years, has included some surprising open doors. i thought it would be fun to tell those stories.

For various reasons, that book just wouldn't write. When asked how it was going, i would often tell people that i felt like a sprinter trying to learn to run a marathon. The things i write are short, a book is long, so i'm not sure how to write a book. Another side note, the sprinter metaphor isn't perfect because it sometimes takes me two hours to write three sentences. At that rate, a book would take several hundred years to write. But every time i walked into a bookstore, something in me ached to have a seat at the table.

It was suggested that perhaps i should consider working with a ghostwriter. i was told that ghostwriters are for people who have interesting or marketable stories but are not good at (or can't be bothered with) writing. This idea frustrated the crap out of me, because writing is something rather sacred to me. And while it does not happen nearly as often as it should, i love to write and i believe it's something i'm supposed to do. Also, the idea of a ghostwriter is strange to me because:

Someone writes a sentence.

Someone else gets credit for that sentence.

No thanks.

And so for years the idea sat, an awkward dream on some back burner. Awkward because there was no update, no progress. It took a while to warm up to the possibility that i could simply be myself, that i could write the way i write, about the things i'm moved to write about. And then it took some more time to realize that perhaps my book was mostly written, that in the nine years since TWLOHA began, i had written thousands and thousands of words, words that i was proud of, words that had moved people. What would it look like to find the best of it, and to put it all in one place?

And so began a journey in reverse, to collect and to remember and to place things side by side. It turned out there were clues back at the beginning, in the days before the story that would change so many things. There were words starting to emerge a decade ago, when i was just a surfer selling t-shirts and boardshorts.

What you hold in your hands is a collection of sprints. Ten years of sprints, and i also think of them as songs. This book represents ten years of life and writing. In that time, i've been all of the following: college dropout, surf industry sales rep, non-profit founder, college speaker, and a person who struggles with depression. This book is how i felt on holidays, those celebration days that have a way of reminding us what's missing. This is what i wrote when famous people died, and when dear friends died as well. There are letters to my mother and stories that i gave as gifts to girls. This is what i wrote when i sold the diamond ring, and when Kyle gave me the jersey with the extra letter in his name. This is what i wrote about the mornings when my nephew Landon makes my parents' backyard feel like the most amazing place on Earth.

This is the book before the one that people were expecting. That one will come with time, maybe even soon, but this one had to happen first. The truth is that part of me felt lost, feels lost. And it's hard to tell a story you don't like. So there was a subplot as i began that backwards journey, back through the last ten years. i'm trying to get back to someplace true, to someone i knew and liked a lot. i'm trying to make sense of my story, trying to make peace with it, perhaps so i can tell it, but more so i can smile. The ache is for a life that i believe in, and this book is brave in ways i hope to return to. i needed to go back, to read these words and retrace the steps, in order to move forward.

All of that brings us to you. i wonder where this finds you. i wonder what you've known and what you feel, what you've found and lost and hoped for. Perhaps there's still time, time for things to turn around, time for us to be surprised. Perhaps there's still a lot of beauty to be found here, and good people too. People to love and people who will say we're not invisible. Perhaps there's everything we need.

So if you feel as if you feel too much, well then you are not alone.

May these words find you like a friend.

THE SALES REP YEARS

(2005–2006)

E-MAIL TO MOM

From: Jamie Tworkowski
Sent: May 17, 2005
To: Janet Tworkowski
Subject: Hi Mom

Hi Mom.

i hope i didn't make you sad. i'm really okay. i think i'm just being super honest with myself, admitting what i see when i look at my life. i love you guys so much. Please know that. i usually come home disconnected from "home" so i usually spend the first few days questioning everything. i really want to pursue writing while i work for Hurley. i have some great contacts, some other avenues i may want to pursue. Between Relevant, Don Miller & Lowercase People, that's a good start right there. i met the editor at Surfing Magazine this weekend too . . . i promise i won't do anything stupid based on being sad or lonely or just for the sake of change. i love you guys and i'm glad to see you tonight, glad to be together. We live in a great place. i don't really know what will happen. It would be cool to surf in Australia and to see the Eiffel Tower next year, but more importantly, i just want to be where i'm supposed to. i want to use my gifts. People are more important than travel. Writing would be cool. My friend Gord says if i write, i will probably need to speak, and i think with some discipline, i could do that. i know it's in me to connect with people. It is easier for me than anyone i know, so i have to think there's something to that, that it might be better served outside of me driving around selling clothes. i know wherever we are, God can use us. Our jobs are not our identities. i want to be a good steward, whatever that looks like. i am pretty sure i will end up here with a family. i'm just wondering about the next little while. i might have to go see some things and say some things . . . Don Miller says that in a lot of ways, i'm where he was, so that's pretty interesting. We shall see. The #1 thing i want you to remember is that i love you!! i am only allowed to dream because you and Dad gave me so much.

Love.
jamie

TO WHISPER AGAINST THIS

To answer an ache. To be some small solution, a piece of change in this new poverty. These reasons place me on a plane, headed for Houston. That i will travel alone from Florida is nothing heroic, only more alive than another three days with those awful images. Something in me says, "Go."

My name is traded for a proud peach wristband, and with ten minutes of orientation, i am officially an Astrodome volunteer. i join a group of seventy to assist in "clothing distribution" but quit quietly when i realize this job is not what i came for. i am not above organizing clothes, but the thing in my chest came for conversation.

At the entrance to the dome, i stop a woman leaving and confess my intentions. It's a strange attempt at legitimacy but she seems to understand. She is a social worker and with a smile she says it should be no problem for me to join the many inside. Another woman from the Red Cross agrees, and i am invited in.

The ocean of cots that fits inside my television is around

me now and i know instantly that this day will stay with me. i am given no agenda but my own: to connect and be alive in this place, to listen and lean against the darkness, and to reach in if possible.

The pain of our poor is being exposed. They have lived long in silence, as microphones keep close to money. We're seeing our humanity now, something insane arriving in this unbelievable circumstance. Dark wind and poison water, hunger and guns; chaos captured by rolling cameras. We're forced to face it, forced to see ourselves.

It's hard to believe that all of this began with a hurricane, a storm given life by a warm gulf sea. The fingerprints of men are everywhere, in solutions and problems and politics, in anarchy and accusations. The response that i will witness today is massive and compassionate. People here and everywhere are moving to meet needs, preparing and serving meals, organizing clothes, offering airplanes and homes and medicine. It's beautiful but cannot contain the tragedy. It's hard to understand that my September Saturday inside this Astrodome holds only a fraction of the truth. A similar structure 300 miles east is filled with nightmares that i cannot imagine. There are signs for the missing here, but i can't hear their voices. The fires of Louisiana are far from me.

The first man i meet is old and warm and quickly kind. He introduces himself—"David, like David and Goliath." He calls me "Jamie, like Jamie Foxx." It makes me laugh and i realize that i will listen more than i will speak today. i'll be given more than i can give. It is a privilege to be here.

Young men from New Orleans are doing calculus on cots, finding inspiration in strange new skies. Boys are being boys, moving perfectly from tackle football to toy soldiers on a small strip of turf. Old men laugh of this display of youth while mothers braid hair and keep children close. One boy smiles bright and points to Peyton Manning's autograph on his Jimi Hendrix t-shirt. The quarterback was here yesterday. Dr. Phil is here today. Bill Clinton and George Bush will be here tomorrow. There are reporters and men with cameras, soldiers and police, doctors and nurses. Men in suits move through, pitching religion while hundreds more live theirs quietly.

It is some strange slice of life, so many characters moving through, me among them. i see so many things: poverty and laughter, rescue and pain. Hope is here too. They are a beautiful broken people. i forget that i'm in Houston, as every conversation is New Orleans. i am tasting that famous blend of history and fantasy, music and mayhem, bright lights and darker things. Beneath banners of business and victory, inside a dome built for pleasure, i sit among ten thousand stories.

Walter is a curious sight, built like a linebacker, leaned over a book and some papers. Stepping closer, i'm surprised to find algebra. "That doesn't look like much fun," i say, hoping to connect. With a smile, he tells me that he loves it. It's what he wants to do. The book's cover corrects me, and i am seeing calculus for the first time. My fear of the great math was enough to move my major a few years back. Walter laughs at this and laughs harder when i tell him that the stuff doesn't exist outside of college classes. He smiles and points upwards, to the huge domed ceiling above us. It is impressive, like something from space, even after forty years. "That's calculus," he says, still smiling. "Calculus built that."

If i listen, there is so much here to learn. Invitations are extended and i join card tricks and board games. Conversations come from men with diseases, mothers with babies, children with smiles. i am introduced as some new friend to so many of them. Today seems a day with no strangers and it's refreshing. There is value in all people, in life, in today, and i say it because they're reminding me. So often i have aimed for privacy and comfort, freedom in finance, but i am seeing something better here today.

Preston is here from St. Bernard Parish. He offers a fast handshake and a sincere, slow smile. We talk for a minute before a neighbor comes to wish him goodbye. The two men have shared a neighborhood for years, but this day will divide them. Their final moment moves me. "We've been at this a long time," he tells his friend. "We're gonna keep on going. I'll see you down the road."

In the afternoon, i go upstairs for a soda. i take a seat in an empty section on the second level. It's my first time away from the floor, and the zoomed-out view puts tears in my eyes. It's difficult to consider that what i am seeing is a situation improved. For so many here, this is rest after rescue, but the image remains unsettling.

Back downstairs, i meet the Pittman family. Like nearly everyone i'll meet today, they are black and poor and very kind. i notice no adult men among them, and one girl stands out. Crystal shares her family's features, but her skin is lighter than mine. She is a black girl in bright white skin. Her nephew notices this out loud. It is an awkward, painful moment. She has light eyes, blonde hair, tattoos on her arms, and legs unshaved. i notice the names of men on both arms and the word "yellow" large across her lower back. She sits coloring quietly, shy and seeming younger than her 17 years. She has my attention, and i wonder silently what pain she's lived and been given to. She is innocent.

On the opposite end of the floor, a gospel choir begins to sing. They are without microphones, forced to compete with all the noise inside the dome. Instantly, i am up and drawn to the music. Their songs are desperation and hope, and when they sing that "Hallelujah" chorus, my eyes fill fast with tears. The beautiful word has always meant mystery and movement to me, and i am feeling it now more than ever.

There is so much that i can't explain on this day and in this moment. i'll be peeling back the layers, trying to understand, for years to come. We are a people in need. The dark wind that moved in New Orleans is here as well. It blows against this building and inside my chest. It's in the cancer that takes the fathers of my friends. The only hope i can think to whisper against this is love—love revealing itself in sacrifice and shelter, finance and food, compassion and community.

This dome built for pleasure has found its greatest game. Love battles loss under championship banners. The seats are mostly empty, but the stakes have never been so high—stories by the thousands, all in need of better endings. Victory has always lived on the field, far from sideline seats and comfortable couches. If tragedy is bigger than a giant building, it won't fit inside your television.

Let the seats stay empty. We should take the field. Love does win, and we're invited to be and build a better ending, alive in all the wonder of a "Hallelujah" chorus.

ZEKE SANDERS: YOU WERE LOVED

i didn't know him well, but this is what i knew: Zeke Sanders was hilarious and kind, small and huge in the same moment. He was humility and rock star, fashion and fishing, alive and encouraging and broken and hopeful and a thousand other things i'll never know. He was simple and complex. He was my friend. Something hopeful in me says he knows now how much he was loved. We will miss his smile, his laughter, his kindness, his tiny jeans and enormous shoes, made for wrestling. We will miss him tomorrow night when we set up, Sunday when we tear down, and Monday morning at Ian's, when it's too quiet. i don't know what else to say. i just have to believe that we are all more loved than we'll ever know. And we're all in this together.

DO QUIT YOUR DAY JOB

(2006–2009)

A few days after Zeke's death, i was invited by my friend Justin to the set of a music video shoot in L.A. It was for the band She Wants Revenge. i was familiar with the band, but that's not why i decided to go. i went because Justin told me Joaquin Phoenix would be directing the video. This was right after the movie *Walk the Line* and Joaquin's award-winning performance as Johnny Cash.

It was a Saturday, and i made my way to a high school in Hollywood, where the video was taking place. The first time i saw Joaquin, i noticed that his arms were covered in some kind of Magic Marker scribble. A closer look revealed these were his notes and ideas for the shoot. It struck me as odd. Clearly, this was a guy who could afford an assistant, and that assistant could carry something like a clipboard. It was an odd sight, but it also felt bold in a way, honest in that perhaps he didn't care what people saw or what they thought. The image stayed with me as i went back to Florida.

i was renting a room from my friend David McKenna in

Orlando. David's story was one of addiction and recovery, and i was getting to know him during a healthy season in his life. His phone rang late one night. It was David and myself and two other friends, standing in his kitchen. He talked for a few minutes, and when he hung up, he invited the three of us to come with him to meet a girl named Renee. It was after midnight, and i had to be up early the next morning, to be on the road for work. i lived with a lot of anxiety and stress back then, always feeling behind in my job, so i remember almost saying no. But the invitation felt important. That turned out to be the night i met Renee Yohe.

What follows is the story that changed everything for me. i remember thinking that "To Write Love on Her Arms" was an odd title, but it somehow felt appropriate. The phrase was a goal. At first it was a goal for one person. Today it is a goal for many. The story would take on a life of its own, making its way around the world, eventually giving birth to what some have called a movement.

Love arrived that year as well. i had met the girl more than a year before, at a Lovedrug concert in Orlando, but it took some time for her to see me how i saw her. She was living in New York City when that happened. The TWLOHA story had become a bigger thing. i had left Hurley to pursue it full-time. And now i had a girlfriend. It was a huge year. At the end of 2006, i bought a diamond ring, a New York City diamond for a

New York City girl, after asking her father's permission on the day after Thanksgiving, in Memphis, where she was born.

Things began to unravel in the days that followed. At the end of seven weeks on the road, on Easter morning after traveling all across America for Anberlin's *Cities* tour, we broke up in her parents' driveway. To this day, it is the most painful experience that i have ever known. "Note to Self" was written in the days that followed. The song i reference is called "Amazing, Because It Is" by my friend Aaron's band the Almost. The song became a friend to me in the months that followed.

TO WRITE LOVE ON HER ARMS

Pedro the Lion is loud in the speakers, and the city waits just outside our open windows. She sits and sings, legs crossed in the passenger seat, her pretty voice hiding in the volume. Music is a safe place, and Pedro is her favorite. It hits me that she won't see this skyline for several weeks, and we will be without her. i lean forward, knowing this will be written, and i ask what she'd say if her story had an audience. She smiles. "Tell them to look up. Tell them to remember the stars."

i would rather write her a song, because songs don't wait to resolve, and because songs mean so much to her. Stories wait for endings, but songs are brave things bold enough to sing when all they know is darkness. These words, like most words, will be written next to midnight, between hurricane and harbor, as both claim to save her.

Renee is 19. When i meet her, cocaine is fresh in her system. She hasn't slept in 36 hours, and she won't for another 24. It is a familiar blur of coke, pot, pills, and alcohol. She has agreed to meet us, to listen, and to let us pray. We ask Renee to come with us, to leave this broken night. She says she'll go to rehab tomorrow, but she isn't ready now. It is too great a change. We pray and say goodbye and it is hard to leave without her.

She has known such great pain: haunted dreams as a child, the near-constant presence of evil ever since. She has felt the touch of awful naked men, battled depression and addiction, and attempted suicide. Her arms remember razor blades, fifty scars that speak of self-inflicted wounds. Six hours after i meet her, she is feeling trapped, two groups of "friends" offering opposite ideas. Everyone is asleep. The sun is rising. She drinks long from a bottle of liquor, takes a razor blade from the table, and locks herself in the bathroom. She cuts herself, using the blade to write "FUCK UP" large across her left forearm.

The nurse at the treatment center finds the wound several hours later. The center has no detox, names her too great a risk, and does not accept her. For the next five days, she is ours to love. We become her hospital, and the possibility of healing fills our living room with life. It is unspoken, and there are only a few of us, but we will be her church, the body of Christ coming alive to meet her needs, to write love on her arms.

She is full of contrast, more alive and closer to death than anyone i've known, like a Johnny Cash song or some theater star. She owns attitude and humor beyond her 19 years, and when she tells me her story, she is humble and quiet and kind, shaped by the pain of a hundred lifetimes. i sit privileged but breaking as she shares. Her life has been so dark yet there is some soft hope in her words, and on consecutive evenings, i watch the prettiest girls in the room tell her that she's beautiful. i think it's God reminding her.

i've never walked this road, but i decide that if we're going to run a five-day rehab, it is going to be the coolest in the country. It is going to be rock and roll. We start with the basics: lots of fun, too much Starbucks, and way too many cigarettes.

Thursday night she is in the balcony for Band Marino, Orlando's finest. They are indie-folk-fabulous, a movement disguised as a circus. She loves them, and she smiles when i point out the A&R man from Atlantic Europe, in town from London just to catch this show.

She is in good seats when the Magic beat the Sonics the next night, screaming like a lifelong fan with every Dwight Howard dunk. On the way home, we stop for more coffee and books, *Blue Like Jazz* and Anne Lamott's *Traveling Mercies*.

On Saturday, the Taste of Chaos tour is in town and i'm not even sure we can get in, but doors do open and minutes after parking, we are onstage for Thrice, one of her favorite bands. She stands 10 feet from the drummer, smiling constantly. It is a bright moment there in the music, as light and rain collide above the stage. It feels like healing. It is certainly hope.

Sunday night is church, and many gather after the service to pray for Renee, this her last night before entering rehab. Some are strangers but all are friends tonight. The prayers move from broken to bold, all encouraging. We're talking to God but i think as much, we're talking to her, telling her she's loved, saying she does not go alone. One among us knows her best. Ryan sits in the corner strumming an acoustic guitar, singing songs she's inspired.

After church our house fills with friends, there for a few more moments before goodbye. Everyone has some gift for her, some note or hug or piece of encouragement. She pulls me aside and tells me she would like to give me something. i smile, surprised, wondering what it could be. We walk through the crowded living room, to the garage and her stuff.

She hands me her last razor blade, tells me it is the one she used to cut her arm and her last lines of cocaine five nights before. She's had it with her ever since, shares that tonight will be the hardest night and she shouldn't have it. i hold it carefully, thank her, and know instantly that this moment, this gift, will stay with me. It hits me to wonder if this great feeling is what Christ knows when we surrender our broken hearts, when we trade death for life.

As we arrive at the treatment center, she finishes: "The stars are always there but we miss them in the dirt and clouds. We miss them in the storms. Tell them to remember hope. We have hope."

i have watched life come back to her, and it has been a privilege. When our time with her began, someone suggested shifts, but that is the language of business. Love is something better. i have been challenged and changed, reminded that love is that simple answer to so many of our hardest questions. Don Miller says we're called to hold our hands against the wounds of a broken world, to stop the bleeding. i agree so greatly.

We often ask God to show up. We pray prayers of rescue. Perhaps God would ask us to be that rescue, to be His body, to move for things that matter. He is not invisible when we come alive. i might be simple, but more and more, i believe God works in love, speaks in love, is revealed in our love. i have seen that this week and honestly, it has been simple: Take a broken girl, treat her like a famous princess, give her the best seats in the house. Buy her coffee and cigarettes for the coming down, books and bathroom things for the days ahead. Tell her something true when all she's known are lies. Tell her God loves her. Tell her about forgiveness, the possibility of freedom; tell her she was made to dance in white dresses. All these things are true.

We are only asked to love, to offer hope to the many hopeless. We don't get to choose all the endings, but we are asked to play the rescuers. We won't solve all mysteries and our hearts will certainly break in such a vulnerable life, but it is the best way. We were made to be lovers bold in broken places, pouring ourselves out again and again until we're called home.

i have learned so much in one week with one brave girl. She is alive now, in the patience and safety of rehab, covered in marks of madness but choosing to believe that God makes things new, that He meant hope and healing in the stars. She would ask you to remember.

HIDING IN HEADPHONES (FOR MEGHAN)

A man with no home is asleep outside a store that sells blue jeans for $300. i am walking by, alone, hiding in headphones. There is a small spot of blood on the man's shoeless foot. There are tourists to my left, and we are seeing the same thing. One of them offers his buddy 50 bucks to kiss the bleeding foot. They both laugh. The awful joke cuts through the song and i feel it in my stomach. i want to tell them terrible words. i stay quiet. We keep walking. We go our separate ways.

i walk to Central Park, the peaceful eye in the middle of that giant skyline storm. Bright-lit buildings lean against a beauty more true, the kind they can't compete with. Progress gives way to what was there before it in the park. Rich men would sell it if they could—they would trade the trees for cash, more cash, more buildings, more rent, but someone wise decided this place needed a park. It is a giant beautiful park.

A couple in love is enjoying a picnic, a moment stolen from some perfect movie. Nearby a woman sits in heated conversation with herself, stuck in a moment, still reaching for something she lost years ago. My path divides them, and i can't shake either scene. i want to be the couple. i want the woman to be healed. i don't know the way to either place. My own heart is heavy and with a head full of songs, i keep walking.

i walk to the new Apple store on Fifth Avenue, its entrance a glass box strange and daring, the store itself underground. i smile at the architecture; i stare at the glass. i check my e-mail and find that a friend's cancer has returned. Meghan. My eyes fill with tears. i consider her kindness, the constant smile, her dreams of change, her hope for Africa and romance and music, dreams for tomorrow and today. She is young and alive and i can't wrap my head around this, the possibility that death might be breathing in her chest now, coming to take her. i don't know what to say. i start to type. i tell her i'm sorry, i say she's not alone, i tell her that my too many friends will be praying. i tell her she's brave. It's all brand-new but i already know she's brave.

i'm reminded what's important, reminded of humanity, this beautiful painful confusing struggle-of-a-thing called life. Suddenly, the store i'm standing in is revealed to be ridiculous. The gadgets, the glass, the celebrity sightings—unnecessary, meaningless. i need to leave. i need to cry and pray. For Meghan, for all of us, "a prayer for the wild at heart kept in cages," in sickness and in health, all alone together and in such great need.

PS: On a hopefully humorous side note: i finally bought that all-black Yankees hat. It's a little too big and i guess i was feeling kinda hip-hop, so i wore it a little crooked for my last few hours in the city. On my way to get a taxi, i walked right past Ice-T (rapper/actor/getting older). He was wearing his crooked Yankees hat. He seemed pretty impressed with me in mine.

NOTE TO SELF

Dear jamie,

The only justice is love. Just let it go. You don't
have to write back. You don't have to explain. This
is not about being right. There is something true
inside the song you can't stop listening to. You
don't feel at home anywhere, but you feel at home
when Aaron sings that song. Someone calling you
a criminal does not make you a criminal, just as
someone calling you a hero does not make you a
hero. Nobody gets to name you. Find your identity
in the one true place. If someone gives you
something, and then takes it back—that's okay. If
someone says something or sees something, and
then they don't—it's okay. Do not be like some
broken lawyer making the same argument over
and over again, always reaching for rewind. Guilt
and regret, those are awful places. You know that.

So don't live there. Do not despair. Do not be afraid. Grace is the interesting thing. Hope.

And God must be a pretty big fan of today, because you keep waking up to it. You have made known your request for a hundred different yesterdays, but the sun keeps rising on this thing that has never been known. Yesterday is dead and over. Wrapped in grace. Those days are grace. You are still alive, and today is the most interesting day. Today is the best place to live.

These things deserve your attention: your family, your friends, the people you will meet today, the strangers with their stories. They say, "We are all in this together." It is absolutely true. That girl with cancer in her stomach and chaos in her mind. She's with us. That guy with tears in his eyes and ghosts in his heart. He loved her, and you could see it. You could see it and you told him that it wasn't his to carry. You told him about grace, and you told him about the song. And you believed it. You were certain of it. So if it's true for him, then isn't it also true for you?

Wake up. You're alive.

Your Friend,
Jamie

PS: And that diamond ring, i know you think
about it a lot. i know you don't know what to do
with it. That ring does not define you. It never did.
Then or now. You can wear it around your neck.
You can throw it to the sea. It doesn't matter. It's
not your name. You are free.

ELEPHANTS (FATHER'S DAY)

This is for my dad and yours, and for the dads we've never met, fifty years ago and fifty years from now. There are some things we can't change, and there are some things we can. This is about the idea that if we're not careful, the days turn into years and our rooms fill up with elephants. This is also about asking those elephants to leave.

i had planned to write this last night—it was Father's Day and i had committed to writing a blog. i thought about it all day, the things i wanted to mention. The basketball game was on at my parents' house, and my dad was sitting on the couch across from me. i had told him we would watch the game together, and i guess i was pretending that if i wrote the blog in the same room as Dad and the game, a case could be made that we "watched the game together."

So the game is on and the day has been good—it was my sister Jessica's birthday and so the whole family was together and she'd opened cards and presents and now we were rooting for Rocco and doing a lot of laughing. It was really good, actually. And i guess i was telling myself there had been some traces of quality time and maybe it was okay for me to zone out and write. . . . After a while my mom and sisters left the room, leaving my dad and me alone and still for the first time in months. The game and the blog were the obvious distractions at hand. The truth is that there was also an elephant in the room. i knew it and i've known it for a long time and it's easy to tell everyone else to say the honest thing and say the hard thing but it's a different thing entirely to say those things yourself. So i wasn't going to. Just gonna try to write the blog, put in some pretend time, and stay hidden in the safety of a laptop, a television, and an elephant. It wasn't the first question he asked but i knew it was coming. He asked how i was doing, he asked about TWLOHA, and then he asked about the elephant.

"Are we okay, you and i?"

i didn't know what to say. Where do you start and it would take a thousand hours and i have to write a blog. It crossed my mind in that moment that whatever i was attempting to write was basically a joke and a lie if i chose it over talking to my dad. The truth is that this conversation was weeks overdue. Some of it was years overdue. So i closed my computer and we talked. We talked about the distance. We talked about the way things had changed in the last couple of years. We talked about depression and money and love and home. We talked about pain. We talked about the way things used to be and why things are the way they are. We talked about the things i talked about in

31

counseling last year. We talked about the things that feel broken inside of us. We talked about the ways we feel alone. We said a lot of things that we had both been needing to say to each other for a long time. Confessions and apologies and questions. Honestly, the whole thing wasn't that hard. It weighed a lot less than the silence of all the days before, all the stuff i'd been carrying around. . . .

Basically we agreed that the things we were saying were big and the whole thing was going to take time—it would be unrealistic to think that talking for an hour would suddenly fix everything. It's a process. We didn't have every answer. We can't fix each other. We are each our own person with pain and a past and choices. But we agreed we were back on the right track. Talking, being honest, saying it mattered, saying it was all worth fighting for. Trying to communicate. We agreed that the goal was to be healthy and to love the other person. i can't fix him and he can't fix me, but we have a lot of control over how we treat each other, how we talk to each other, how we make time for each other.

Love is a thousand things, but at the center is a choice. It is a choice to love people. Left to myself, i get quiet and bitter and critical. i get angry. i feel sorry for myself. It is a choice to love people. It is a choice to be kind. It is a choice to be patient, to be honest, to live with grace. i would like to start making better choices.

It is one thing to stand on stages and write blogs and spend all my time talking to strangers about hope and love and community. If i have learned anything in the last couple of years, i have learned that it's a lot easier to talk about loving people than it is to actually love people. It is easier to talk about community than it is to live in community. Honestly, i mostly suck at both. i am good at being short with people, and i have gotten really good at being quiet.

When i die, i hope the people close to me will say they felt i loved them. The rest of it is bullshit if i miss the boat on that one. My dad needs to know that i love him. My mom, my sisters, my friends, the people i work with: They need to know i love them. And i would like to be the sort of person who loves people unconditionally. The sort of person who loves people even when they hurt me. When they offend me. When they embarrass me.

The alternative has not been going well. The alternative is that i set up a bunch of hoops and i say, "Jump through these and you can earn my love. Be exactly who i want you to be and do exactly what i want you to do and you can earn my love." Strange and broken attempts at control. They have not been working.

Basically, there's things i don't like in my own life and i don't know how to fix them (or i'm too lazy) and i end up telling everyone else how to live. i am not very healthy, but somehow i pretend to be the absolute authority on what everyone else is doing wrong—finger always pointing, advice and frustration pouring out of me. Again, it hasn't been working.

As for the original point . . . You have a life. You have a story. You have your past and your pain and your dreams and your future. Perhaps you have a dad. i would be so bold as to say that your dad probably has a lot to do with the stuff i mentioned above. Dads are people, and people tend to do a lot of different things. Great things, beautiful things, horrible things. At some point, some more than others and for a million different reasons, people tend to make mistakes. Our dads were once children—our dads had or have dads—we forget it but it's true. So they had dads and their dads were people too and their dads probably made mistakes as well. My point is that it's all connected, and the older i get, the more i realize that life is really fragile.

> *It seems we humans carry the shortcomings of our fathers.*
>
> —Jeff Foxworthy

Father's Day is a strange day because the word "father" means different things to different people.

"i love him."

"He left."

"He died."

"He's here but he's never really here."

"He's good."

"He used to be good."

"i used to be good."

"i never met him."

"He doesn't understand."

"i saw him ten minutes ago."

"i saw him ten years ago."

"i've never seen him."

"He hasn't been the same since _____."

"i haven't been the same since _____."

"He's great. He's my best friend."

"i wish i could tell him _____."

"i wish i could show him _____."

We want to say we're sorry. We're sorry for the broken stuff in your life. We're sorry for the places that hurt. We're sorry for the questions that won't seem to go away, the places you feel stuck.

These words won't solve everything. It would be great if life worked that way, but i don't think it does. Perhaps this is a moment to consider your own story, to consider your own pain, to consider the sources, to consider some solutions. For some of us, it's a reminder that we have much to be thankful for, things to hold on to, things worth fighting for. For some of us, it's a reminder of things we hope we can begin to let go of. This will certainly be a fight as well.

You're not alone in this. If yesterday was a hard day, you weren't the only one who felt that way. Maybe there are things you need to say. Maybe there's a letter you need to write, an e-mail to send. Maybe it's going to take a long time and today you just need to call a friend and begin to be honest. Maybe things are really heavy or it's just too painful. Maybe it's time to sit across from a counselor. (For what it's worth, i did it for the first time last year and it helped me a ton.) Maybe it's time to find some help. Help is real. Hope is real. These things are possible. You're not alone.

The thing about the idea that you're not alone is that it doesn't do us much good if it's just an idea. We have to do something with it. It's like having no money and then someone hands you a check. You have to take it to the bank. You have to do something with it. Maybe hope is like that. Maybe community is like that. Maybe relationships are like that. We have to choose these things. We have to say they're real and possible and important. We have to say some things out loud. We have to choose to believe that our story matters, along with the stories of the people that we love.

About thirty hours ago, i made a choice to close my computer and i made a choice to have a conversation. The conversation wasn't easy and these words aren't easy but the good news is that there is freedom to be found in all of this. My heart is less heavy today. The elephant is no longer in the room. i know he's gonna try to come back because that's just how life is. Elephants show up where they don't belong and they try to stay forever and they ask us not to say a word.

It's okay to tell the elephants to leave. It might take a long time—it is certainly a process—but i think you'll find that it's a better way to live. And don't worry, you don't have to go alone. You were never meant to.

WE STILL DON'T KNOW WHAT LOVE MEANS

I've been listening to Ray LaMontagne for the last couple of years. Ray is a brilliant songwriter who delivers stories in something like a deep, smooth whisper. He has that golden voice, but i think it's his honesty that i connect with even more. His songs seem to be born from questions and pain, and if i myself am honest, i think i connect with this because i am a person who thinks a lot about pain. i wrestle with the busted stuff in my own life and in the lives of the people around me. i have a lot of questions.

It is for all of the reasons above that some friends and i drove 500 miles from Florida to Atlanta to see Ray LaMontagne play on a Saturday night a couple of months back. We parked and made our way excitedly to the door, and as we took our place in line, i heard it:

"You're going to Hell."

The man's voice was loud and unkind, directed at everyone arriving at the show. He shouted about "fornication and homosexuality," angry answers to questions no one was asking. We later learned the venue was originally a church, the loud man not a fan of the events now taking place. In the first moment i was shocked and then i was sad and then i was walking towards him.

"Do you think this is working?" i asked.

i figured he would be excited that someone actually wanted to talk to him, and he certainly seemed prepared for an argument. Instead, the yelling guy told me that i would need to talk to a different person, pointing towards the younger man to his left. (The yelling guy needed to keep yelling.) Now, this whole thing surprised me because i had no idea that these people had assistants. i guess the kid was learning the ropes, hoping to be prepared to yell on his own within the next year or two. . . .

i told the kid that they needed to stop, that they were only doing damage, offending everyone. i told him that people respond to love, and that i could hear no love in their shouted judgments. His response made me more frustrated, and after a brief back-and-forth, i rejoined my friends in line and entered the show.

It took a while to calm down and let it go. In theory, the yelling guy and i believe some of the same things. We're on the same team, you might say. But i believe in a God who maybe doesn't scream at people the first time he meets them. Evangelism aside, screaming at strangers seems like a horrible marketing plan. i believe in a God who places a great emphasis on love, a God who loves people and asks His followers to do the same.

By the time Ray took the stage, i was able to enjoy the show. The best music is the kind that moves you, reminds you you're alive, takes you on a journey. i smiled through the opening "You Are the Best Thing," imagined during "Empty," and remembered during "I Still Care for You." i had been hoping all night to hear a song called "Jolene," and so i smiled again when its opening chords arrived as the encore.

The song is a story song about a man lost and looking back on a broken relationship. You can see it from start to finish and the chorus echoes the words "I still don't know what love means." It is a confession, and something like a question. Something in me stirs each time i hear it—there is freedom in honesty and those are words i can sing myself.

And it hit me during that encore that i wished the shouting man could have heard Ray LaMontagne sing "Jolene." i wish he could have attended the show he chose to protest. i don't know how hearing happens—how certain things move and change us, but i wished it could have happened to the guy outside.

i think i went back to him in my mind because he is also the reputation of the Church. We are known to the world as something like the guy outside. We tell people how to vote and think and live. We shout our judgments. We are quick with our answers and slow to confess our questions, maybe slower even still to meet other people in theirs.

A shouted "You're going to Hell" is an awful introduction to a God who desires to love and know His children. Ray had my attention with "I still don't know what love means." i can relate to that, and i can't help but think that a lot of other people can as well.

And it's interesting that all of this happened on a Saturday night, because Saturday nights give way to Sunday mornings. Some people stay out late, hunting for meaning and answers in songs and bars and a thousand other places, because they're certain that our Sunday mornings would only be more like the shouting stranger. But what if we were known as a people in true pursuit of love, a people committed to representing it well? What if we were known for constantly showing up to wrestle the needs and questions around us, and what if we took it so far as to be honest about our own?

HAPPY BIRTHDAY

i like birthdays. i like them more for other people, but i'm glad we celebrate them. At the heart of it is the opportunity to tell someone "i'm glad that you were born," which is also to say "i'm glad that you're alive." Those are powerful statements. The world would be a different place if we lived that way, if we said and expressed these things, more than once a year.

i hope TWLOHA can be something like that, an attempt to say those things more often, to say that we are thankful for life and stories and certainly you and yours. i hope that we can be something like a gift, something like a favorite song or some show that you remember, some piece of hope or life or strength to hold against the walls when they feel cracked or falling. i hope we can be a reminder that life is worth fighting for, that your friends and family are worth fighting for, that love and beauty still happen, that change still happens. We'll only ever be part of the process, words on a screen in the middle of the night—i hope they find you like a friend. A t-shirt pulled from your drawer early on a tired silent morning—i hope you feel less alone when you look in the mirror. i hope it reminds you of community, that you're part of a bigger thing. i hope it sparks some conversation that brings change like a fire on the coldest night.

You'll need more than us. You'll need more and better. You'll need other people. You'll need people to help you process, people to help you let go, people to help you remember what's true, and people to help you forget what's lies. You'll need the stories and advice of people with gray hair or white hair or no hair at all. Don't buy the lie that suggests they have nothing to offer or nothing to say—they were young once too. They are stories still going, and they've seen the places you will go. They've been stuck at times as well, just like you and me and everyone.

You'll need coffee shops and sunsets and road trips. Airplanes and passports and new songs and old songs, but people more than anything else. You will need other people, and you will need to be that other person to someone else, a living breathing screaming invitation to believe better things.

We're saying the story doesn't end here, that the air in your lungs is there for a reason. Perhaps we're all in the business of better endings, you as much as us, the business of redemption. Yours and mine and all the characters around us, and perhaps that bigger thing. i'll steal from Bono here and tell you that i believe we're far from alone in this, that God's been at this for a long time, this business of buying things back, making things new. If this is starting to sound too churchy or spiritual, i'll simply say that i believe God gives a shit, about your life, about your story, about your pain. And if those possibilities feel too far or they just sound weird, then rest now and we'll get back to people.

We give a shit.

The darkness wins too often. Broken things build themselves in silence. People feel alone. People give up. People talk about this stuff like it's math or they don't talk about it at all. So what are we doing? Why an organization? Why the shirts? Why did a group of young people put their lives on hold and move to Florida a week ago? Why would they trade everything they know, all their normal comfort and quiet, for a crowded house and endless hours of this word "community"? Why would they want to join a conversation most people run from?

We're trying to fight for people with kindness, with words that move, with honesty and creativity. We're trying to push back at suicide with compassion, with hope. We're pointing to wisdom, pointing to medicine, saying that hope is real, help is real. We're fighting for our own stories, our own friends and families, our own broken hearts. We're saying there's nothing we can't talk about, nothing off-limits. We're kicking elephants out of living rooms, making room for life.

You. It's about you. This is for you. It's crap unless it moves you, crap unless it connects with your story, meets you in your pain, reminds you of your dreams, reminds you what's possible.

We're still alive, you see. You and i on this night that's never happened before. Spread out across a giant circle, winter on one side and summer on the other, day and night the same. And then it moves and turns and changes. Things are always changing.

We are glad that you were born.

We are glad that you're alive.

Don't give up. Don't give up on your story. Don't give up on the people you love. Hope is real. Love is real. It's all worth fighting for.

CAPE CANAVERAL TO NEW ORLEANS

There is a family headed west on I-10 right now. This is for them.

Part of it was the place, this Canaveral condo, this house so much a home. i remember sitting with Byron in this living room five years ago, me on the couch and him on the chair across from me, me all filled with questions, always bringing him my pain, because he would listen, because he was brilliant but more because he cared. He listened for more than an hour, while i talked through my tears. Eventually, in a quiet moment, he shared that he had some news of his own. His girlfriend, Amanda, was pregnant. They had been close to breaking up but now she was pregnant with his child. i remember not knowing what to say but finally asking how he felt and i remember him saying that people make mistakes but maybe God does not.

Isabella Pearl was born months later, her middle name a picture of redemption. There was no shotgun wedding, no cheap whispered promises, only questions and patience and pain and hope. It was a season of uncertainty.

A wedding eventually came, some more months later, after time apart and after time together, after all their searching. Byron flies to Boston, they drive to New York, he takes a knee on the Brooklyn Bridge, asks for her forever. On the same trip, he has coffee with a man whom he respects, a man he's met only once before. Byron talks about his life, the surprises of this season, the reason he's in town. After an hour together, the man says, "i feel like i'm supposed to give you this." He hands Byron an envelope, Byron opens it an hour later at the airport. Two thousand dollars. (There are people who invest in stocks, and there are people who invest in stories.)

The wedding came when they were ready, when the promise could be true, for love is a choice much more than it is magic. They moved the couch out of the living room and got married with the sliding glass door open, next to sea and under stars on New Year's Eve. i said a few words, about not knowing who i would be without his friendship. i can't remember if i said it, but i hope i said that i believe in their story.

Baby Eve is born. Byron takes a job with TWLOHA, first as an assistant, soon as our director of operations. He shines. It's hard to tell his life from his work from his dreams. i mean that in the best way. We rent a bungalow. Interns begin to arrive. They watch football at his house. They eat dinner at his house. Baby Eden is born.

i could say other things—that we ended up on different pages for a time, that i am difficult to work for, that i am not the healthiest person. It's hard to navigate the waters of ego, pain, and pride. It's hard to have a single honest relationship— easier to say "community" from a stage, easier to be busy than known. We hurt each other. We let each other down.

Some weeks go by. Weeks with silence. We're both offended. He decides it's time to move on. He quits a good job in an economy where people don't quit jobs, where people don't make choices because they believe in them, because they live one time and want to do it well.

He and i are fine now. Time has a way of putting things back where they belong. Love has a way of breaking the silence.

Byron and his family headed north and then west today, to make a home in New Orleans. To give themselves to a city as it comes back to life, to raise the girls in a place rich in history and poverty and diversity, to be part of a bigger story. Byron is going back to school. His is that brilliant mind that will never stop asking questions, never stop learning. There is not a lot of money, not a certain plan. Oh, and Amanda is pregnant again. ("You're kidding me" and "No way" have been common responses.)

We said goodbye last night. This is the guy who introduced me to my favorite band, the guy who taught me it was okay to ask the questions you aren't supposed to ask, to say the honest thing, to be creative. He suggested that there are things more valuable than money, that maybe people matter most. He talked about the value of a place, a good idea, something true inside a moment or a song. . . .

It crossed my mind to play it cool. i cried about it last week, broke down in front of a roomful of people—our entire team and even some strangers—it would be easier not to cry this time. Besides, everyone else said their goodbyes without crying. i'm 29 years old. i should have my shit together by now. i should be able to say goodbye without crying. i should be able not to need people.

Or maybe this is okay, maybe this is the way that i was made, to feel things, to say things. i don't know. i just know that i started to walk away and then i stopped. And we've been down this road enough, done enough life together, that neither one of us had to say anything.

He told me once that he believed friendship might be life's greatest gift. What an amazing thing to feel known and loved, to feel understood, to walk through life with another person. i remember that it all felt true when he said it and i know that it has stayed with me.

i eventually told him through tears that he will leave a great space, that things won't be the same, that he can't be replaced. He said the words meant a lot, because it's something we can't tell ourselves, what we mean to other people. We hope we do, but it's powerful to hear it, significant to receive.

i forget which one of us said it first, but we have agreed and said for years now that there are things in life worth crying about. (We added to this list: things worth screaming about, questions worth asking, trips worth taking.) It was true last night and i suppose it's true again right now.

i don't have a magical ending except to say that i hope you get to experience this sort of friendship, this gift that Byron talked about, this thing that just might be a miracle. i hope you get to say these things and hear these things. i hope you get front-row seats for a story as good as Byron and Amanda's. And part of me hopes, for you and for myself, that you get to live that sort of story.

New Orleans is a better place today.

THE NEW YORK YEARS

(2009–2011)

When Byron left, i knew that things had changed. It was the end of an era, and it was time for me to go. i was dating a girl in New York and we were very on and off. We were actually off at the time but starting to talk again when i decided to move. i had already committed to an apartment a few blocks from her when i asked, "What if i moved to New York?" i had found a place on the corner of Fourteenth Street and Third Avenue, two blocks from Union Square. i signed a three-month sublease and ended up staying two years. It's my favorite place i've ever lived.

New York is so many things. For someone who has a hard time being still, it's easier there, because you can be still inside a storm. i loved sitting in Stuyvesant Square or Union Square, i loved walking just to walk, i loved noticing the characters on the subway. New York is a melting pot and there's something healthy about that, rich and poor together, different colors— different lives all side by side. i loved it and i miss it and i flirt with moving back.

My parents grew up in Mineola, on the west end of Long Island, just outside the city. That this book is being published by a New York publisher isn't lost on me, because New York means a lot to me. It's part of the story i was born from, and it's part of mine as well.

ALIVE AND BRIGHT IN BROOKLYN

This story begins in the greatest city in the world, on the six-teenth of September in the year 2008. It was the beginning of the season known as fall.

It's hard to say who found who. He was in Brooklyn to watch a friend play music. He saw her from across the room but didn't know that he had known her. She recognized him, not from any sort of fame, but from her memory. They had grown up in the same simple place.

She said his name. He was not the usual bar-and-darts suspect, but that was the scene in which she found him. She would tell him months later that he seemed free in that first moment, alive among friends and a drink and a smile, there in her New York. It was a break from planes and lesser places, and she would later also say that she liked that he was busy.

She had grown up, was a woman now, stunning and com-fortable, and he could not look away. There was a rare and special sharpness about her and she made it all seem easy. She was safe in her skin, safe in this city, even in a season of transition. She was simple in the best way and happy in the best way. She was very much alive. He wanted, even in those first moments, to make her laugh and make her smile. He wanted to be close to her and certainly to know her.

He said they should take pictures, to say the night had happened, to say they both had been there, alive and bright in Brooklyn. She thought it strange but she agreed. They jumped into a taxi. They ate breakfast in the middle of the night, among strangers and friends on Manhattan's Third Avenue. He didn't want the night to end. He did not want to sleep.

He asked to walk her home. She said no. He asked again. It's doubtful that she ever said yes but he did walk her home, down Third and at some point crossing over. He would have walked to Jersey. They talked in front of her apartment, and it crossed his mind to kiss her—he knew he couldn't, but he hoped to. And he hoped to see her again, in either of the places they had known.

They said good night, and as she made her way upstairs, he jogged the six blocks back to the place that he was staying. It was in him to worry, to wonder if he was safe at this hour in this place, so he jogged because of fear but he also ran it laughing. This woman and this night, the surprise inside of all of it, it meant he was alive.

They could not have known it all that first night, the friendship that would grow in evenings on the phone, the hours gone to laughing. They couldn't see it as it happened or guess what it would become, but there was a chemistry, something sparked and shared, a balance in their differences. She would teach him stillness and laughter, how to enjoy things and appreciate, a meal or friend or show, and the puppies in the park. He would show her patience and kindness, wanted her to feel seen and known, appreciated and beautiful. His dream became to love her, and to be loved by her.

Love is a choice as much as it is magic. Magic comes in moments, but choices stretch out over time. We make them new each morning. In the first fall, they were magic. Then the seasons brought their storms, as seasons always do. Summer brought a winter. There was crying and silence and he would go away to change, for sometimes we have to lose a thing to find it.

In her New York now, there is talk of fall returning, cool air and boots and tights and certainly the colors. There is hope in him that they will see it all together. Love is a story and theirs is now and happening, uncertain but hopeful, like any good story. Fall suggests it's possible to change, that things can still be new, alive, and bright again, alive and bright like Brooklyn.

VISIT TO BUTLER UNIVERSITY

One of the great privileges of recent years has been spending time on college campuses. Doors keep opening and invitations keep coming and we love to go, to lead a conversation that we believe in, to talk about things that don't normally get talked about—this problem of pain that perhaps you and i relate to.

To be honest, i'd never heard of Butler University. i had to Google it to find out where it was. (Turns out it's in Indianapolis and has been since 1855.) We expected to be there back in February, but the snow came blowing through and so we had to reschedule. Our February 10 date was traded for March 31 and, in the days between, winter gave its place to spring. There were also some basketball games, and the underdog Butler Bulldogs had become the smallest school since 1985 to make it to the Final Four.

We arrived last week to all of this and to students lounging on green grass, floating Frisbees under easy sunshine, and to all the hope and wonder of a Cinderella story. Our gang included myself, Denny Kolsch, Aaron Moore, and Ryan O'Neal from the band Sleeping at Last. None of us had ever been to Butler. We didn't know anyone who was attending or had previously attended Butler. In short, we had no connection to these people or this place outside of this surprising moment. And yet, we were swept up in the whole thing. The scenes unfolded like some good movie. We texted friends to say "We're at Butler." We wondered if there might be time to buy Butler Final Four shirts. As we made our way downstairs to start the event, i wondered why exactly we were smiling. Officially, none of this had anything to do with us and yet we could not stop smiling.

i wondered about association. Was it just that we felt close to something special? That idea felt true, and yet i wondered if there might be more. . . .

After my first winter in New York, i learned that spring makes sense only because of winter. You notice the warm sun on your face because it hasn't been there.

And then perhaps it's true that we are wired to root for the underdog, to cheer the unlikely ending, the win where loss is likely. Those words would certainly apply to Butler's men's basketball team. They would play in the championship game that night, once again the underdog, up against the storied Blue Devils of Duke.

Our night at Butler stayed with me. i started thinking it was less about the weather and less about basketball. Perhaps the heart of the matter, the magic of the moment, perhaps it had more to do with people. People sharing in the wonder of it all, suddenly so much to smile about, so much reason to celebrate. And for them, these folks we shared our night with, it was not some random story moving through some random place—this was them and theirs. This was home—Butler's blue now a color they belonged to, the mascot bulldog something like a friend. And suddenly, a whole nation was tuning in, saying that it mattered, saying that this story was significant. And because this Butler story was also theirs, then perhaps they mattered too.

And perhaps the most amazing part was they were in it all together. Making signs and painting faces, shouting together at televisions and lying around in the spring. Together. Because none of it would have been the same alone. There is a joy that comes with sharing. It's true when you're small and it's true in college and it's true when you're old. And it's true with losing just as much as with winning.

Our event began with a few words from a student named Brandon, a kind and capable guy who helped organize our being there. Brandon offered a sobering introduction. We were there, everyone in that room and in the glory of the moment, one year to the day since a Butler student named John Burton took his own life. And so the night took on a different sort of weight, the lightness of the season and the games crashing into the heaviness of an absence caused by pain. Ryan sang the words "You were meant for amazing things" and i wondered if that was really all we were there to say. We go in hopes that people stay alive and fight to live, so that they might arrive at a day when those words feel possible and true.

We live a thousand different stories, you and i. We live so many different seasons and who can say when winter or victory or spring? Perhaps all we can do is go together, win and lose together, because both are better that way, because we deserve a people and a place and a color and a team.

THIS MEMORIAL DAY

Please remember the ones who can't forget, the soldiers for-ever trying to get home, trying to let go, to be okay.

To soldiers and to the friends and family of soldiers, we pause to acknowledge you today, to say that you matter. The things you've seen, the things you've lost, the battles that you fight, the dreams that steal your sleep—may we never call them small.

And we apologize today, for the ways that we forget, for the ways that we are selfish, for our lack of understanding. Perhaps the ones who've never been there, we can't begin to compre-hend words like "war" and "fight" and "home." We don't know what they weigh and what they cost.

To the ones who fought for peace and freedom, we pray those things for you. We pray rest and hope and healing, and innocence again. We pray for people who will listen and the strength for you to speak. May other people know you, walk with you in the questions and recovery. May you get the help you need, the help that you deserve.

Today we say we see you, and not only as a soldier but also as a person. Someone not unlike us. You are significant. You are not forgotten.

Finally, humbly, thank you.

FLOWERS TO THE SEA

A town is so much more than just a place. People come together to live and tell their stories, united by history and
family; they gather over food and work and sport. Moments
hilarious or terrible inspire nicknames that carry on through
life. It all adds up to something bigger. Virginia Beach is a
surfing town, and i am writing from that place.

Zeke died five years ago, his death a suicide, a choice and
moment just like millions more, except the kind that's all too
final, the kind that leaves no room for others. First Street, this
ocean, this place, is where his ashes were scattered. Men who
love the land are given back to the land, but surfers do it different. Surfers paddle out, hold hands, and make a circle, spread-
ing ashes along with flowers across the surface of the water.
And then we scream and splash and say goodbye. Perhaps we
scream because it's impossible, because hearts aren't made to
break. Zeke's friends did this on a freezing cold January day in
2006, two hundred people in the water and just as many
standing on the beach. It was a scene that made the news.

i wasn't there that day, but i was there yesterday, for the 5th Annual Zeke's Lil' Rat Surfcus, a unique surfing competition meant to make kids smile. Creativity often comes from suffering and this is also that, Zeke's friends and family doing their best to create something special in his honor, beauty born from pain.

We woke up early to assemble tents and prepare for the day. The kids arrived and the contest began at eight. i watched as Zeke's mom, quiet and humble, worked to make sure everything was perfect for them. Every boy and every girl got an official contest t-shirt, black and white so that they could add the colors. She set up a table with fabric markers so that they could make their art. Zeke was always drawing and painting, so this made perfect sense. She brought bubbles and water guns to let the kids be kids, to see them play and smile. This is crucial because we get older and we forget how to play. Pain and worry come to steal our smiles. Mothers, the good ones, they fight to help us keep them. Zeke is gone but his mother is still a mother.

Midway through the morning, she walked away without announcement, away from the buzz and noise and laughter of the contest. She walked alone, away from the tents, across the sand towards the rocks that form the jetty. She walked with flowers, and my friend Nicole told me they were sunflowers, because you give sunflowers to the people you truly love. The kids near us cheered and screamed for reasons unrelated, the surfers surfed, and the announcers added noise. Zeke's mom moved slowly across the rocks, stopping at the very tip. She threw the flowers to the sea.

"She does this every year, and also on his birthday and on the day he died," Nicole told me as we watched.

Zeke's mom paused for just a moment and i watched her walk back and i watched her wipe her eyes.

Two hours later, i sat down in the empty chair beside her.

"Today must be bittersweet for you," i said, after small talk and some silence.

"Every day is bittersweet," she replied.

We sat for some time, often without words, under a burning summer sun. i didn't offer answers because i had no answers to offer. When we did talk, we talked about family and pain and change. We talked about her wonderful brilliant grandson and we talked about my sisters.

Zeke was my friend when we both worked at Hurley. Nicole was Zeke's girlfriend, and i've had the chance to get to know her over the last year. i came to Virginia to support her and to meet the other characters, the friends with nicknames, Zeke's family, Zeke's hometown. i didn't know it when i bought my ticket, but i came to watch a mother remember her son, to say in her own way, that she remembers, that he was significant, that she is still his mother.

Every single kid who surfed in the contest left with information about TWLOHA and a TWLOHA t-shirt. There was no epic speech, but it meant something to me to know that every kid left that beach with a bag suggesting "Hope is real. Help is real. Your story is important."

The hope in all of that, the reason TWLOHA exists, is to keep the flowers from the sea. Death will come for all of us but let us fight to live. Let us bury our mothers, for they should not bury us. And if it should happen the other way or if it already has, i hope you get to know the privilege of seeing them remember. i hope you get to sit with them in silence, the silence simply honest, and neither of you alone because the other one is there.

In Loving Memory: Zeke Sanders

I HOPE YOU FELT THE FIREWORKS

It's funny that i don't remember loving the Fourth of July as a kid. Funny because it's become one of my favorite holidays. And this may sound bad but, for me, it's not really about loving my country. Don't get me wrong—i love America, i am grateful and proud to live here, grateful for my freedom and aware of what it cost. But if i'm honest, that's not the thing i think about when i watch fireworks exploding against the night. i think about wonder and i think about hope.

i've watched them with the TWLOHA gang from the windows of a van as we made our way laughing through the cornfields of Illinois. Last year in love and on a boat in Florida, this year beside a thousand strangers on Eleventh Avenue in Manhattan, all of us peeking past the skyline. There was one Fourth of July a few years ago where i just went to sleep. Awake meant pain and so i just tried to sleep.

Perhaps you have to have a little bit of hope to believe that beauty can be found, to believe that life does come back, that something can surprise you. And maybe hope and wonder are somehow related. Maybe wonder feeds hope and hope feeds wonder. You see something beautiful and it reminds you that it's possible to see something beautiful.

We got in a cab last night and laughed at our requested destination. "We want to see the fireworks," i told the driver, hoping he would know the place. He took us to Forty-Ninth Street and Seventh Avenue and we walked the rest of the way, joining the giant crowd on Eleventh, as far west as we could go.

The grand finale came as a stream of constant color, thunder shapes dancing and painting the sky. And it struck me that we were all there by choice and by chance. We were there to watch the wonder, no one telling us what to do or how to respond. In the final minute, as the skies exploded, we all clapped and cheered. We had become one thing. It was a significant moment for me in my new home, not forever but for now. This city never stops. People call it a monster and talk about feeling swallowed and alone. People constantly give up and go home with broken dreams, feeling invisible, feeling forgotten. Last night i saw it pause. i saw thousands of people walk west with hope to catch a glimpse and then i saw them see it. i can't say why each person went or what their story was before. i can only tell you that i went to feel alive. i went because it's too easy to forget, to believe the night sky is always only black. i went to stand next to my friends in hopes that we could share this and remember.

Last night, i hope you felt the fireworks. i hope you saw the wonder when the skies filled up with color. And in that moment, i hope you were reminded that it's possible, that beauty still happens. We don't just live in books awake and dreams asleep. We are living our stories, you and i, with dreams inside us undeniable, with love to give and people to walk beside.

i hope for you what i hope for myself—that we might keep walking west and looking up, that we might see something wonderful.

INCEPTION

U pside-down buildings and special effects, that is what i went for. These things will win awards but they are not the reasons you should go. You should go for the humanity. You should go because you will relate to the people stuck in moments, the people living with ghosts, the people trying to get home. You should go to be reminded that our lives are also stories, the best of which involve someone fighting a battle. In *Inception*, the enemies are guilt, regret, pain, and shame. The movie serves as a reminder that these enemies unchecked will haunt and hunt you always. Thankfully, the movie also serves as a reminder that people need other people, that our stories and our battles and our dreams, these things are meant to be shared.

i went for what i saw in the previews, fantastic things pushing and falling and exploding around the characters. i left thinking about the things that push and move in me, my ghosts and wars and dreams. The movie suggests that we are most alive and most awake when we are dreaming. And while a case could be made that it is speaking to the dreaming that occurs when we're asleep, perhaps it's true or even more true of the dreams we dream awake.

Inception suggests that there is much at stake; our hearts and our children and the air in our lungs. i am 30 years old. i don't feel old but some days it sounds old when i say it out loud or see the number written down. It's easy to buy into the idea that "dreaming" is a silly word for children, that "battle" means the military and that ghosts are not real. *Inception* felt like an invitation to remember that there might be more to the story, a world we don't see but one that is connected to the days we wake to.

There is certainly much at stake. i don't know your story or your dreams or the things that steal your sleep, but i know they matter. i hope your story is rich with characters, rich with friends and conversation. i hope you know some people who will carry you, and i hope you have the honor of carrying them. i hope that there is beauty in your memories, and i hope it doesn't haunt you. And if it does, then i hope there is someone who will talk you through the night and remind you of the promise of the sunrise, that beauty keeps coming, that there are futures worth waiting for and fighting for, and that you were made to dream.

THE ONLY KIND THEY FEAR

'm reading a book called *The Fountainhead* right now. It was written by Ayn Rand and it's blowing my mind. There are two main characters, both architects, though they do the job for very different reasons. One, Howard Roark, is an artist. He dreams of the buildings of the future, buildings unlike any that exist. He knows the gifts of vision and passion, but he is forced to face the challenges that come with those. "Vision" means seeing things before they exist, which means running into folks who can't see what you see, or they tell you it's wrong or simply not possible. Peter Keating gives a speech at graduation. He is the A student, the one "most likely to succeed." Success is what drives him, though not success that's self-defined. He wants to be great in the eyes of others; he wants to impress people.

The book opens with Roark getting expelled from architecture school just before graduation. He is expelled not for drugs or bad behavior. He is expelled essentially because his work—his ideas and designs—are too radical. He is asked mostly to re-create the greatness of centuries before, to do what's been done. But in that request, he is asked to be something he's not. And his heart, his gift, is too strong and too sacred. He won't trade it to please people, especially people he doesn't respect. The work is deeply personal for him. It is not for money, not for others; it is an extension of himself, and with that, it must be true. When Roark is expelled, the Dean tells him that he must value the client above all else, that the architect exists only to serve and please the client. Roark responds with this: "I don't intend to build in order to have clients. I intend to have clients in order to build."

i used to worry a lot. When i was younger, i worried about the future and money and girls (especially girls). And then when TWLOHA started to take off, i worried about how to keep it going and how to make it last. People said it wouldn't, and this made me worry more. Growing up, i got along with everyone and had very few enemies. So it was weird when, as TWLOHA began to build and grow, people i didn't know began to say ugly things about me online. They said i was in it to be cool, in it to get rich. People i thought were my friends recycled rumors. In short, i saw the best and worst of the Internet and the best and worst of people: passion and communication, cynicism and hate. And in the alternative music scene, if you want to call it that, i feel i've seen the best and worst as well. We've been embraced—this is our fourth summer on Warped Tour—and we've had the privilege of sharing our message on tours with Anberlin, Bayside, Switchfoot, the Rocket Summer, and the Almost. The fans of some of our favorite bands have become believers in the work we do. And then, at the same time, we have our critics. People love to hate, love to be cynical, love to tear down the thing that rises.

It used to bother me a lot, used to steal my sleep, when people would say mean things or things that weren't true. i didn't understand it, and it hurt my feelings. But i've learned to focus on the work and the heart of the matter—the people in the balance. i can't control what people think, especially people who say things without even bothering to look at our website. Is the work authentic? Is it poetic and hopeful, creative and brave? Does it move people, does it serve to push folks back from edges? Does it point to hope and help? Are we being careful with the money that we raise, spending it wisely and doing as much good as we can with it? These are the questions that deserve my attention, and, thankfully, i am not alone in those questions. There's a whole gang of us answering them every day.

In the process, i am more and more aware of my own story. i'm facing my own questions and struggles, wrestling with my dreams. My hope for both of us, for you and me alike, is that we won't settle; we won't walk away from what we love because it's too hard or because people are mean or they don't see what we see. Whether it's songs or sales, whether you want to be a doctor or a teacher, in life and work alike, i hope you get to do the things you love. It's easy to be a critic, easy to tear things down, easy to be blind. It's a braver thing to build, to create, and to surprise.

We're more than four years into TWLOHA now. The time has flown by and the story still surprises me. i meet people who say, "Your website saved my life," and it's them who keep me going, keep our entire team going. We also hear the whispers, things like, "They don't actually help anyone." i can't say why it is that one work is met with two very different responses. Some see it, some believe it. Others call it crap. But i'm learning more and more that some of those folks, the meanest loudest ones, know very little about our actual work. They don't want the truth; they just want to break the thing that's building. With that, i'm learning to ignore them, that this is not for them, it isn't theirs to steal. We do this work, we build this thing, because we believe it to be true, because we know the need is real. Because people walk alone, people live in pain. People choose to die or they live lives without living. TWLOHA is for them, built with hope that they will find it as a hand to hold, something real and something true.

i am early in *The Fountainhead*, still a lot of pages left, and i hope the same is true about my own story. Perhaps you can relate to feeling in the middle, to having questions in the air. i don't know about you, but i hope to live a good story, to see things invisible and watch them come to life. The critics will probably always be there, calling us crooks or fools, but we should just keep going. They can't see what we see, and they are not the thing that drives us.

i'll leave you with this from Roark's hero Henry Cameron, who he eventually works for: "You love your work. God help you, you love it! And that's the curse. That's the brand on your forehead for all of them to see. . . . The substance of them is hatred for any man who loves his work. That's the only kind they fear."

It's better to be true than to be cool. Be yourself. Do what you love.

RING THE BELLS

We'll ring the bells that lead you home
'Cause the only truth I've ever known
Is that nothing ever hurts us more than love
So circle up your best of friends
And we'll celebrate the way it ends
At least we live tonight
At least we live tonight

i am writing to tell you about a song. The song was not written by a famous artist. The band is not signed to a major label. i have listened to the song twenty times today. i listened to it three times in a row this morning, borrowed headphones plugged into a borrowed computer in a borrowed office. i cried for ten minutes straight. It is an awkward thing to be a grown-up crying in an office, especially someone else's and especially during business hours, and yet the thing i heard in the head-phones came louder than the fear or shame i felt for crying. There was the sense that i was hearing something impor-tant, something that felt true to the deepest place in me. Who can say why we love something or feel something? i am cer-tainly no authority, but perhaps it starts with truth. There is something about hearing or seeing or feeling something that is true.

My friend Steven McMorran lives in Los Angeles. He lives with his wife, Danielle, and their adorable baby boy, Aiden. They chose Los Angeles and they remain in Los Angeles be-cause there are songs inside of Steven. They stay also because of the people around them who not only believe in those songs, they know the cost and weight of the songs. They live in a humble apartment that though close enough in miles, is far from Malibu and Mulholland. They have made it a home, made with things that can't be measured in square feet. It has been my privilege to get to know them over the last couple of years, to learn their stories and to be loved by them. When i spend time with Steven and Danielle, i am certain that i am loved beyond anything that i could ever explain or earn or deserve. i am certain also that my friends are living a sacred story worthy of love songs and fight songs, a story rich with victory, defeat, sadness, forgiveness, laughter, depression, re-demption, passion, pain, and hope.

"Ring the Bells" is the title track on an EP that came out today. The band is called SATELLITE, and my friend Steven is the singer. The song is a love song and a fight song and perhaps also a prayer. It is urgent and beautiful and powerful, and i believe it because i have seen my friend Steven talk about his wife and son without blinking.

THE GIRL WITH THE HYPERCOLOR HAIR

Her birthday arrived between the seasons. She had spent the summer busy in the north and would soon go east to start another chapter. He hoped her summer had been good beyond the work, hoped she'd know more evenings in the park, moments with her daughter, and moments with herself.

He knew her only from fractions of days at the start of the summer, a dinner early one evening, and then an afternoon spent celebrating the engagement of her sister. In telling her what it was like to be 30, he used the phrase "taking inventory." He paused to ask if she knew what he meant. She paused only to smile and asked if he thought she was stupid. (He did not.) She spoke unafraid of turning 30, seemed not to buy the lies or fears believed by others. She said that her twenties had not been easy and spoke with hope for these new days.

She said she would soon be going to Toronto to make a movie. She mentioned something about the movie involving a taxi. His schedule would place him in Toronto while she was there—he was booked to speak at a conference. He joked that he would wave at every yellow car. She said it might be easier just to call.

In Canada, he asked if she liked birthdays. She said that birthdays made little sense aside from love, without a person to share them with. He knew that feeling but had never heard it put to words. He really liked her answer.

He asked if she enjoyed her job. She said she did but not the cost, not the things it stole and not the things it added. And she didn't say it, but he imagined that she enjoyed the work itself, enjoyed the process and the craft. He knew she loved the theater.

She was stressed at the time, only just arriving but already having to go back to New York to fix the color of her hair. She apologized for the silliness of it all, an apology he found not necessary, for if it mattered to her, then certainly it mattered. He sent her a note in the night and another in the morning, said she was lovely in a way that color couldn't steal. He said that everything would be okay, and she would be home before she knew it.

She thanked him some days later and said that things were getting better. She said that she was like the Hypercolor sweatshirts people wore when they were kids, colors changing constantly. He confessed to never owning one but smiled at her words.

On her birthday, he hoped she felt loved beyond circumstance, alive and celebrated even far from friends. He hoped for her a peace and freedom that could not be taken even on the days she liked the least. He hoped her life now and always would feel something like a trip well traveled, not that it would be easy but that it would be worth it. He hoped whatever dreams she had, that she would get to see those dreams.

And though he did not know her well, he felt glad that she was born. And so he said that on her birthday.

HAPPY BIRTHDAY.

FOR DAVID

L ast week i hit a wall. It's the feeling that while the story i get invited to tell is impressive to some, the story that i actually live is not. i feel lately like i live a story about a guy who rides on airplanes and in rental cars and hopes the pillows in the hotel rooms are comfortable. The smiling irony in the whole thing is that i get invited to come and tell people that they need people, but then i don't really have people in my own life. i have access to it, but community is a thing you have to choose.

So last week i started to feel the weight of too many airports and too much time away from home. But i was already committed to going to an event. In fairness, this event was a gathering that i was honored to be part of, and it would mean the chance to catch up with friends. But there would also be a lot of folks i didn't know, which meant there would be a lot of first-day-of-school moments where you answer the "What do you do?" question and hope that people like you. (These moments are not fun for introverts, especially tired introverts who wish they were at home.) But instead of impressive people attempting to impress one another, i found a group of people willing to be human, willing to be honest and vulnerable in admitting the broken parts of their stories. There were confessions of mistakes and questions and doubts. There were grown men with tears in their eyes, willing to go there in front of people they didn't know.

There was a man with cancer in his body, and, with his wife at his side, he spoke of the pain of the last year, the fear and embarrassment of the seizures that find him now. He spoke of the kindness of his friends, the miracle of the thing we call community. He spoke with love for his 5-year-old daughter, and there were questions that did not require words.

We were invited to pray for him, to put our hands against his body, and to ask God to heal him. i have no idea how that works, why God fixes some people and lets others die. i don't write much about faith because i feel like almost all the words have been abused. i've become embarrassed by most things called "Christian," but i still believe in a God who loves people. Anyway, we were invited to pray, and i knew i had to go. i made my way close to him, to where i could reach through the crowd to touch his right arm. Different people prayed out loud and i don't remember the words, but i remember crying and i remember the feeling of wanting this man to be okay.

i walked back to my chair, tears falling down my face but without shame. And it struck me that this moment had happened inside a gathering that i had feared might be a shallow celebration of folks with lots of answers. Instead, the moment that meant the most was the one with no answers at all. It was a group of us meeting one among us in his enormous question. i go to so many things where it's experts and leaders and public-speaker people. There is a strange circuit for folks the world calls important.

This is not a "Come to Jesus" blog. It is simply a confession that with all that i've seen in the last few years, all the events i've been invited to, and all the people whom i've met, i am less and less impressed by "impressive" things or people who are presented as having things figured out. i am impressed by people who are honest and kind. i am inspired by moments of vulnerability, moments of confession and compassion, moments where someone makes it clear that they are a person in need of other people and someone else makes it clear that the first person is not alone.

We've done some winning in the last few years. There have been some bright moments and surprising open doors. MTV and *USA Today* and *Rolling Stone*. CBS News. None of it meant as much to me as that moment praying for that man, when crying was the most appropriate response, because there are tragedies in this life that deserve our tears. i will not forget the privilege of standing in the small sea of strangers, reaching into sickness and mystery and hoping God might be real and hoping that He loves His children.

Be loved. Be known. Love people and know people. Be so brave as to raise a hand for help when you need it. Make friends and make sure they know they matter. Be loyal to them and fight for them. Remind them what's true and invite them to do the same when you forget. If you do some losing or you walk with someone else in their defeat, live with dignity and grace. It is a middle finger to the darkness.

In the event we live to be old, i doubt our last days will find us aching for success or achievements. i doubt we'll ask for bigger names or Internet followers or virtual friends. If influence comes, then let it come, but it was never the point of the story. We will look back and smile at the moments that were real, the people who knew us and the people we knew, the relationships and conversations, the days we walked together, the story that we told. We will consider the moments when we were allowed to show our beauty and our mess and the miracle moments when we were embraced by people who loved us even at our worst. And they loved us not for any sort of fame but simply because our stories had joined somehow and that miracle of friendship had taken place.

An hour after the prayer, it was time to say goodbye. This man named David, who i now consider a friend, told me that on his darkest nights, he wears a TWLOHA shirt to bed. He said he does this to remember that he's loved.

> *Friendship is a diminishing of distance between people.*
>
> —Keith Richards

FROM DAVID KUO:

> *"Snapped a picture of you the other night. I can't really imagine what your life is like but imagine it can be lonely and exhausting and sometimes dark. Love from us Kuos"*

FROM JAMIE:

> *"Interesting timing. i just wrote a blog about meeting you, called 'For David.' Would love to know what you think. i'm happy to adjust or change it if needed."*

FROM DK:

> *"More tomorrow, but as I lie here, with Kim sleeping next to me, wearing my TWLOHA shirt, it is a beautiful thing to read—intimate in the way that being known allows . . . requires. . . Vulnerable because it is so true, so captures it all . . . there was in those days something sacred. So thank you for*

writing and being so vulnerable yourself. Don't change anything. Use the story whenever and wherever you like. We Kuos love you."

(NEXT DAY)

"Dude. You can really write. What are you gonna do with that gift?"

FOR PEOPLE WHO SUCK AT THANKSGIVING

The idea of a day where we reflect on the things we're thankful for sounds easy enough. i'm writing this on a computer, one of the many luxuries in my life. There is much to be thankful for, but the truth is that i tend to do the opposite of what this holiday is meant for. My thoughts gravitate to whatever's missing, whatever's lost or broken or painful. My heart worries and fears. There is plenty to be thankful for, but those are not the scenes i stay in.

i wish i was better at these days. The days where the whole family comes over and you hug and smile and catch up on what the year has been. i wish i was better at being present. i'm tempted to say that i wish i was better at being happy. That has been one of the great mysteries for me and perhaps you can relate. And it's not that i don't have plenty to be happy about. There is more than plenty. My life is absurd in terms of how privileged it is. i've been all over America this year. i've been to Australia and Europe, and i've lived in New York City. Insert whatever word you choose: Blessed. Fortunate. Lucky.

So what's with all the pain? What's with not being able to sleep at night? What and where the heck is "home"? Is it possible to be healthy? To be patient? Why do i feel things so deeply? Perhaps you can relate to some of those questions. So i guess i'm writing this for three reasons.

1. We (this includes you) deserve the space to be human. To be real, to be honest. To be a mess, to cry, to laugh while crying, to do whatever you need to do. Now, my guess is the idea of going there in front of your awkward Aunt _____ probably doesn't sound like much fun. So maybe you don't. Maybe you do your best today. To be present. To think about the other people in the room. To ask questions and to try to care for the people around you and to let those people care for you.

   But it goes back to the first part. You deserve the space to be human. Family chooses us but we get to choose our community. Our friends. Our support system. We were meant to be known, to be loved, to be in honest relationships where we can be carried and where we can help carry.

2. i wonder if it's possible to get to a place of being thankful for your story, for the dreams that feel fractured, for things we loved but lost. i wonder if it's possible to get to a place of believing that we are shaped by all of it, that we

are stronger and wiser for what we've walked through. What if the things that ended—the things that broke and break your heart—what if it was the end of a chapter but the story keeps going? What if life comes back? What if love comes back? What if you would not be who you are and you would not know what you know if not for all those sleepless nights?

i'm starting to believe those things, that the best is yet to be, that life comes back, that the dreams that live inside me are there for a reason, that life is not just a tragedy, not just a story about losing. It is also a story of surprises and grace and redemption, of conversations and moments that feel like miracles.

i share this quote every night onstage, but it's taken on a new meaning lately. i've been reflecting on it offstage, sharing it with friends and believing it more than ever:

> *I suppose that since most of our hurt happens in relationships, so will our healing, and I know that grace rarely makes sense to those looking in from the outside.*
>
> —Paul Young, *The Shack*

3. Don Miller says we have to fight to remember that "other people exist." We are surrounded by other people and

that each person is living a story and every single story has questions and pain of its own. If we only ever think about ourselves and our drama, we will miss the price-less privilege of stepping into the stories around us.

We have to fight to not get lost in our own pain. We have to fight to remember the good, the things we love around us, the things not lost, the things that we are thankful for. Don't buy the lie that your story is just a tragedy. And don't buy the lie that you are the only character in your story.

Today seems a good day to start.
Happy Thanksgiving.

MILLION-DOLLAR DAYS

(2011–2012)

DEAR VALENTINE'S DAY

Dear Valentine's Day,

My friend Don wrote a blog about you today,
and his blog suggests that you used to look a lot
different than you do today. He says that you are
the product of a poet and that before this poet's
pen, you were not a romantic holiday.

   i think i would have liked you more back then,
whenever that was. The truth is that you really
bother me now. i think you bother a lot of people,
honestly. You show up every year right after
Christmas. You turn the windows pink and you
sell your diamonds on the radio and i think i've
gotten five e-mails from 1-800-FLOWERS in the
last three days. i'm not sure how you got so much
power.

   Don't get me wrong. It's not that i don't like love.
i love love—i think it's the best thing that happens

on the planet. It's the biggest dream inside me. But i bought a lie somewhere along the way. i bought the lie that says i'm not alive if i'm not in love. i bought the lie that says if i love someone but then they stop loving me or they start loving someone else, then i must have no value or power or worth. i bought the lie that says if i'm not in love, then i'm as good as dead. And if you believe that lie long enough, it makes a giant hole. It makes a hole so big that no one person could ever begin to fill it. Not even a princess. Believe me, i've tried. To fill it with a person, to fill it with beauty, to fill it with all the things you sell.

But i don't think it works that way. Bono says his songs come from a God-shaped hole inside of him. He's my favorite singer, and he has a lot of things. He has great stories and a wife and kids and plenty of money. But in spite of all of those things, he says he still has this hole and he says that it's the reason that he sings.

i've been thinking lately that maybe i've confused girls for God, a different one every year or two, since the first day of junior high. And man, that is a lot of pressure to put on someone, to make them God. That is a ton of power to hand someone.

Especially when they're just a person. A person with questions and flaws and pain of their own.

So maybe there's a war, inside of me and for me, and maybe my heart is the opposite of small. Maybe it's the opposite of cheap and empty and alone. Maybe it's sacred and enormous and wild. To make a long story short, i think i've given you way too much power. i let you scare me and i let you name me and i let you tell me what i'm worth. i don't want to do that anymore.

There are dreams inside of me and those are mine and my guess is that they're there for a reason. But for all the days like now where the dreams are asked to be only dreams, i'm gonna keep getting out of bed. i'm gonna keep living my story. i'm gonna believe that there is reason and purpose, and power in my life. i'm gonna believe that i'm alive inside a story bigger than my pain, bigger than everything missing.

It crossed my mind to try to ignore you, to try to go to bed early and wake up when you're gone. But i changed my mind. i am part of a gang in Florida and we're getting together tonight. We're going to open our computers and we're going to choose to believe that words are powerful. We're going to do our best to tell someone something true. We're going to ask people not to give up on their stories.

Valentine's Day, i don't hate you. i don't even blame you. Perhaps you did not name yourself. Perhaps you are the product of hundreds of years, hundreds of thousands of broken people and a million God-shaped holes.

The truth is that we're all living love stories.

REINDEER

My brilliant photographer friend Jeremy moved from Nashville to Los Angeles recently. Because he's brilliant, he had the idea to turn his move into something bigger. Friends should come along, and he would document the journey. But he also felt the trip should have a purpose, something beyond just transporting boxes from his old house to his new one. He called to ask if i had any ideas. i said we should make stops along the way to ask people about their fears and dreams. He could take pictures of folks holding up their answers. Jeremy invited a few friends to join us for the journey. i ended up having a crush on one of the girls. The following took place at the Grand Canyon.

She said, "You shouldn't be so hard on yourself."

i asked what she meant.

She explained and i didn't cry but i came close so of course she asked me about it. i said i didn't really know but the trip had caused me to feel things more than usual. Maybe it was the driving and the lack of sleep.

"You're amazing and i want you to own that."

i told her i was looking for checks that i could cash.

She said lots of people are amazing but it doesn't mean that they belong together.

i didn't roll my eyes but i basically rolled my eyes.

On our way out, we saw a bunch of elk but none of us knew what they were. i thought they were reindeer but the people in the car next to us said they were elk. It would have been really cool if they were reindeer.

"HAVE YOU EVER STRUGGLED WITH SELF-INJURY?"

H ave you ever struggled with self-injury?"
A girl asked me this during Q&A at the end of last night's event at St. Louis University.

People often ask if i've struggled with any of the issues that TWLOHA deals with (depression, addiction, self-injury, suicide). i have no problem admitting that i am a person who struggles with depression. i've been through seasons of counseling, and i have been on antidepressants for the last two years.

But this girl didn't ask about depression. She asked specifically about self-injury.

It would have been easy and honest to simply say "no."

i've never cut myself or burned myself.

But i knew there was a better answer. It felt important, and so i want to share it here.

i believe that self-injury is a form of coping. It's using pain to deal with pain. People are after relief and release when they do it.

If that's true, then the heart of the matter is not the behavior.

It's the reason for the behavior. The problem is pain. So perhaps the million-dollar question is, "What do we do with our pain?"

We all answer that question in our own ways. We respond to our pain. We cope.

Drugs and alcohol.

Pornography and sex.

Anger and violence.

Eating and not eating.

Friends and community.

Counseling and treatment.

i've never taken a razor blade to my skin, but i've certainly hurt myself. i've hurt myself and i've hurt other people in dealing with things that i've felt haunted by. i've never cut myself, but i don't think i'm so different from someone who has.

So maybe it's not black-and-white. Maybe it's not, "Do you cut?"

Maybe it's, "We're all human and we all encounter loss and pain and longing and questions. We get stuck and we get lost and we buy lies."

Maybe the question is, "Okay, so what do we do with that?"

And maybe it gets a whole lot easier when we simply begin to go there, to see it that way, to admit we're human, to admit we all have our stuff. Maybe from there we can begin to relate to and understand one another. And maybe then we can begin to walk together towards healing.

TELLING GHOSTS TO GO

What does it mean when something is haunted? What exactly is a ghost? Is it when something from the past refuses to leave? Is it when something dies but doesn't go?

It's easy to talk about haunted places. A haunted house. A haunted building. We smile at those stories. We get excited. There is no stigma, no shame. But what about haunted people? Isn't it true that, as people, our lives can become haunted things as well? The past can haunt the present. The past can steal the future.

Isn't that what most of this is about? Something painful in our past? Something breaks or something dies and in living with the pain, we begin to live with ghosts. And by our choices, we either ask the ghosts to leave or we help them make a home. If we can talk about haunted buildings, then we should be able to talk about haunted people. We should be able to put a hand up and say, "i'm not doing well" or "i need some help" or "Can we talk?"

Maybe we begin to ask the ghosts to leave when we begin to

ask some other folks to join us in our haunted places. In the broken parts of stories. Our messes and our questions. To meet us, to know us, to help, to care, to listen.

Maybe we begin to help our friends become unhaunted when we let them know we're not afraid of their pain. When we ask to really know them. When we ask to see inside. When we do our part to go beyond the distance and the smile, deeper, to "Who are you?" and "How are you?" and "Are you okay?"

i have been a haunted house. i have had things die but stay and i didn't know how to make them leave. And there were certainly times i didn't want them to leave because they were beautiful. They were no longer real but they were beautiful. They were bridges to brighter days. i thought they were my dreams.

Reality is the best place to live. Reality is where healing happens. In the honest light and by the voices of our friends.

We all have our past. We all have our pain. We will all know ghosts from time to time. But if our life is like a building, then we should open our doors to let some people see inside. Into our darkest places, into those rooms that hold our fears and dreams, we will begin to go together. Friends with hope like candles, telling ghosts to go.

THE PATIENT TELLING OF
ANOTHER PERSON'S WORTH

A young sales rep, an introvert unorganized and so an odd fit for the job, began the life of visiting stores in the business of surfing. His job took him all across the state of Florida but it was the trip to almost Alabama that stood out in his mind. This was for reasons of distance and time, but it was more than that as well. The drive to Florida's Panhandle felt like something nearly sacred.

The trip, which he made some thirty times over the course of eight years and 40,000 miles, was anchored by a small chain of surf shops. These stores seemed to matter and for reasons beyond business. They seemed to tell and celebrate a story, the story of a man and his family, the story of a people and a sport, and a story even bigger.

At one of the shops, there was a picture on the wall, one among a sea of them, but this one somehow shining. It was the shop owner's daughter, beautiful and talented. She may have been just down the street in his first and early visits, but she would move north and later west, to places dreaming people go to chase their dreams. And so in all his different visits, he didn't ever meet her.

For him, there was always something about this place that she was from, and the drives it took to get there, something about being that far from home and was it worth it and what was his life supposed to be? He was always asking questions. He was nearly always restless.

Years later, sitting in a movie theater on Sunset Boulevard in Hollywood, he would see her on the screen, at first inside an old Western photograph and then alive and moving. Her beauty was impossible and something in him hoped to know her. He knew little about her, of who she had been or who she was becoming, but he knew something of the folks and place she came from. And he knew he hoped to know her.

The same afternoon he saw the movie, he found a way to send a note. He mentioned the story and stores. He mentioned the kindness of her father. She responded almost instantly and then his phone rang and then, somehow, she arrived and stood before him. He had met the women called the most beautiful in the world. Upon meeting her, he knew that he had never met anyone more beautiful.

She shared that it had been her hardest year, a year of loss and losing, and yet a year with good as well. They found in each other a friend. He knew the way he saw her, the way she caused him to remember and also to believe. He did his best to swallow all of it. She was so lovely that he had to look away at times, but overall, as a thing new inside his life, he knew and would eventually tell her, that he could not look away.

She was something so alive, sharp and sure and kind, rich in ways beyond money. She liked to laugh and felt things deeply. She was driven in her work and yet knew also where she came from. She was aware of her story and the stories that she shared in. She loved her father with an extraordinary love, which continued even in the distance of his passing. She had a young son, and upon seeing them together for the first time, he felt the awe that comes with watching something wonderful. Her son was innocence and joy, and his laughter gave the day a different meaning.

He had loved the Mumford & Sons song "Timshel" since the first time that it found him, but the song meant something more as he began to know her. It seemed a gift from God, written for this woman and this time. He told her and she said it was the song that got her through those initial painful days. He never heard "Timshel" again without seeing her inside it. His surfs at County Line, and the drives to and from, all of that became Church.

He went to New York. She said she hoped he might cross paths with her brother, said she worried for his heart after the loss of their dad. When on his way to surfing the very next morning, her brother walked 10 feet in front of him; it felt like something straight from Heaven. There was no heavy epic talk, but they surfed together, and they did a bit of laughing.

He liked the brother and of course it makes one feel good, to cause a funny man to laugh.

She brought out the best in him, reminded him of parts of his own story, woke up things he had forgotten, his dreams and who he hoped to be. He did his best to be a kindness in her life, a blessing, not a burden. This chance to get to know her, to be good to her in moments—he counted it a privilege. She had an incredible confidence, a safety in her skin, and yet he knew her heart was broken. In a moment brave and rare, he sent a letter in the night to say the truest thing he'd say that year. That he would go away to war if it meant her heart could be restored. She responded with his name, over and over. He wondered what it meant, if perhaps he was in trouble. She said it was a good thing.

They would find later that their fathers had been friends in the 1970s, both men in the business of surfing, both men good and kind. And they would find that in her visits to the beaches just above Sebastian Inlet, she stayed one street away from the one that he was raised on, Flamingo versus Cardinal. After meeting her, he would wonder many times how it was he hadn't met her sooner. There was certainly no answer but he was grateful it had changed.

She was with him on the biggest night and moment of his life, invited as his guest. There was the pressure of a million dollars and a television audience. A lot was on the line. For him, it was the world just to have her in the room. The speech was him, who he was born and wished to be, and while of course he hoped some stranger might be touched by it, he hoped as much that she would see him in that moment.

She would ask him later the same night, speaking through a smile, why he was so nice to her. The question came as more of a surprise than any million dollars. He smiled silent. He fumbled over words and she pointed out the irony: The public speaker couldn't speak. It crossed his mind that there was now much more at stake.

She called herself a mess. He responded unafraid. He said if he could do anything, it would be to sit across from her. He said the things inside these pages. He said that love was the patient telling of another person's worth, and he hoped in time to show her.

WELCOME TO MIDNIGHT

Five.
Four.
Three.
Two.
One.

The ball drops and fireworks. Resolutions are made.
People scream and people kiss and is it possible to change?
Is it really truly possible to leave the past behind?

Welcome to Midnight.

Another year comes to a close. Another year begins.
With a moment in between.
Why the fuss?
Why the fame and fireworks?
Is it more than hype? More than something else to sell us?

Is there something to this holiday? Something true inside it?

Because isn't there something inside us that aches for change . . .

Dreams it to be possible . . .

To let go.
To hold on.
To leave it behind.
To start again.
To be new.
Is it possible?

If you're reading this, if there's air in your lungs, then you're alive today tonight right now.

And who can know how long we have here. . . .

And is it a gift? Was it ever a gift? Did that ever feel true or could that one day feel true?

Are there things to fight to live for?

Moments and people. Weddings and children and all your different dreams.

Love.

Is your life more than just your own?

And are there broken things you were made to fight to fix?

Broken families, broken friends . . . Injustice.

Will you move for things that matter?

Wouldn't it be nice if change took just a moment?

Wouldn't it be nice if it were that easy?

Midnight and we're new. Midnight and the past erased. Midnight and we're free.

It seems to come slow. It seems to be a surgery.

Forgiveness. Healing. Sobriety. Letting go. Starting over.

It seems to happen slowly over time.

One day at a time, the choice made new each morning.

Will you fight?

Will you fight to be healthy?

Will you fight to be free?

Will you fight for your story?

Will you fight to get the help you need?

Change takes more than a moment, but maybe there's also something to this celebration of a moment, something to the way it speaks to us, something to the way we fear it, and dream it to be true. Maybe it's the most honest moment of the year.

It's possible to change.

Welcome to Midnight.

Here's to the possibilities.

MOTORCYCLE

R un."
That was his friend's advice.

"She's a man. She's a lion."
"You just showed up on a white horse."
"She wants a motorcycle."

He didn't own a motorcycle.
He had never even been on a motorcycle.

"i'm a mess," she told him.
"i'm not afraid," he told her.

You have my attention.
i know you want a motorcycle or you will think you want
one for a while.
Well, i don't have one.
But i have an unusual heart.
And you can have it if you want it.

JASON RUSSELL IS MY FRIEND

Jason Russell is my friend. i reached out to him a few years ago, as TWLOHA was starting to take off. i was a fan of Invisible Children, and it seemed we could learn a lot from them, and i could learn a lot from him. Like IC, TWLOHA was born from a story and the surprising response to that story.

Jason and i have been friends ever since—he and i, as well as members of our team and members of the IC team. As the world has seen, Jason is brilliant in his talent and creativity. Personally, i also know his kindness and compassion. Jason has been there for me in difficult times in recent years and even in recent months.

After working on TWLOHA over the last six years, i can say there is much that i am thankful for and very proud of. There have also been moments and seasons that were deeply painful: Dealing with criticism and people saying things about TWLOHA and me personally that were not true. Dealing with constant travel for events. There have been times i felt close to a breakdown. There have been times i was supposed to speak on behalf of TWLOHA but our team didn't let me get on the plane to go. They said i needed to take care of me, needed to make helping Jamie a priority. i have gone through two seasons of counseling and i have been on antidepressants for nearly three years now.

i share all of this not for pity or some strange confession. i share all of this because mental health is a real thing. The things we talk about—people needing people, people needing help at times—i believe these things to be true.

Life is fragile. Life is complex. We are capable of great good. We are capable of madness.

i don't know the details of what happened yesterday in San Diego. i don't know the truth. In some ways, perhaps it's not important. i know my friend needs help. i know he needs a break. i know i can't begin to know the whirlwind he has experienced over the last two weeks—the attention, the popularity, the criticism, the exhaustion. . .

i believe in Invisible Children. i believe in their KONY 2012 campaign. i want to see Joseph Kony, the leader of the Lord's Resistance Army, caught and brought to justice. i want to see lives saved. i want to see children in Africa and around the world raised in safety and in peace.

If you want these things as well, then please continue to support Invisible Children.

IC exists to end a war in Africa.

TWLOHA exists to say that there are wars inside all of us.

The goal is peace, in Uganda, in Congo, inside you, inside me.

We are all a people in need.

We are not perfect. We are not machines.

We make mistakes.

We need grace. We need compassion.

We need help at times.

We need other people.

And that's okay.

MOTHER'S DAY

Thank You for ignoring the doctors when they told you to stop trying to have kids.

Thank You that you kept dreaming your dream.

Thank You for loving Jessica and Emily and me.

Thank You for loving Dad, in sickness and in health.

Thank You for all you've sacrificed. You have traded so much to give us a better life.

You gave up horses for a sea you didn't need. And that sea, it's been my home.

And my church since ours exploded.

Thank You that you still believe in God.

Thank You for your innocence.

Thank You for the way you ache for peace.

Thank You for quietly working tirelessly, day and night behind the scenes my entire life.

You are the most selfless person i know.

Thank You that you look at our website more than anyone i know.

Thank You for praying for my wife.

Thank You for believing she exists.

Thank You for your laughter. i know no better sound.

Thank You for helping me sleep when i was 5 and also 25.

Thank You for seeing the best in me when i was not my best, and when i could not see beyond my own pain. Thank You for believing in me. Thank You for believing in the simple bigger story, the too-many surprises, the way the dots connect. Thank You that you see it when i don't.

Thank You that your hope for me is no award and no achievement. Thank You that you simply hope to see me smile. Thank You that you ask if i'm okay when you have a feeling that i'm not.

Thank You for loving me.

Thank You for loving my sisters.

Thank You for loving my Dad.

Thank You for loving Baby Landon!!

Thank You for loving so many people over so many years asking nothing in return.

Your heart beats inside me and i count it no small thing.

i Love You.

i am proud to be your son.

Happy Mother's Day.

THIS IS WHAT THAT STICKER MEANS

Last night in Colorado, a young man walked into a movie theater and took the lives of innocent people. As of now, twelve people were killed and many more were wounded.

We are shocked and saddened by this news. Our hearts and thoughts and prayers are for the family and friends of the people who were in that theater last night. We are sorry beyond words. We ache with you today.

We don't know the story of the shooter. We don't know what could lead a person to do such an awful thing.

Today we learned that his parents live in San Diego.

There is a car in their driveway.

There is a TWLOHA sticker on the back of that car.

We don't know whose car it is or how the sticker got there.

But we know what that sticker means.

It means that millions of people struggle with depression, addiction, self-injury, and suicide. It means that the majority of those people never get the help they need and deserve. It means that what we do with our pain—how we respond to it—

matters. It's one of the biggest questions we get to answer in this life.

We believe it's possible to change. We hear from people taking brave steps towards hope and help and healing. We hear from people sitting across from a counselor for the first time, people stepping into treatment and people picking up the phone to call a crisis hotline. We hear from people pursuing sobriety and stability. We believe that great help exists and we know the first step is often the hardest one to take.

If you're struggling, please talk to someone. It's okay to ask for help. People need other people. If someone you care about is hurting, talk to them. We know it's not always easy, but it could be the thing that changes everything.

We don't know the story of the sticker on that car in San Diego. But we know it sits before a home that must be filled with questions and shame and heartache. And so that home will not be excluded from our love. As we think and pray for the victims, for the many people hurting today, we will consider them as well.

Our job now, those of us simply observing today, shocked by this awful news, our job is to love people. When it hurts. When it's awkward. When it's uncool and embarrassing. Our job is to stand together, to carry the burdens of one another, and to meet one another in our questions.

This is what that sticker means.

WHAT I FEEL VS. WHAT I KNOW

i feel sad more than i feel happy.

i feel stuck more than i feel free.

i feel defeated more than i feel accomplished.

i feel i should have found love by now.

i think about it every single day.

i confuse girls with God.

Because it seems easier to know a girl than a God.

Seems easier to hand everything to a girl.

And we see ourselves as whatever we believe the
    most important person in our life believes
    about us.

So of course it fucks with you if they walk away.

i feel stuck in the best and worst moments that i've
    known.

The million bucks and the silence that followed.

But what is true?

What do i know?

i have a lot to be thankful for.

Mom and Dad and Jessica and Emily and Baby
Landon.

They're healthy and they love each other and they
love me.

i have amazing friends. Old friends and new.

Mark. Ian. CJ. Phillip. Josh. David. Kyle. Steven.
Byron. Chris. Chad. Tyson. Gord.

Jason. Jon. Dustin. Don. Gabe. Eric.

Friends who want to know me and want me to
know them.

i get to do a job that i believe in. Most people don't.

i have the opportunity to make a difference.

A lot of people would give anything for that.

i am healthy and i am young and there is air in my
lungs and a shining sun outside and a sea as
well and a story still going. And i'm allowed to
be honest.

So do not despair.

For there is more than what we feel.

There are things missing in every single room.

But there is even more not missing.

So don't be blinded by the ghosts.

Don't let them glow brighter than your friends.

Don't let them glow brighter than your family.

Be present.

Fight to be present.

Don't live only in your head.

It's lonely and it's dangerous.

Put your phone down for a few hours every day.

Talk to people. Look someone in the eyes and be honest and invite them to do the same.

Read a good book and watch a great film and put a song on repeat and remember who you are.
Keep dreaming all your dreams. And perhaps as well some new ones.

Go to counseling if you need to go to counseling.

Take your own advice.

Take care of yourself.

Take care of the people who you love.

Tell them that you love them.

There is much to be thankful for.

DAVID McKENNA WAS MY FRIEND

Before this website or Facebook or wherever it is that you're reading these words, before this organization or movement or a story called "To Write Love on Her Arms," there were three friends in a small house in Orlando in 2006. It was David McKenna's house, and Renee Yohe was there because of David McKenna's story and even more because of his heart. Renee was in the middle of addiction and depression, trying to find a way out. Renee connected with David because he could relate, because he had been there, because he wanted her to be free.

i was the roommate, a sales rep not wired for sales and a surfer trying to find a home an hour from the ocean. We were perhaps an odd pair, as David and i dressed different, listened to different music, drove very different cars. And yet i found in him a friend. Not just a friend but a brother. The magical depth and commitment and knowing that one cannot explain. We laughed hard and often, had great talks, and rooted for each other.

As far as the five days went, Renee stayed clean and stepped into treatment. David was the leader all the way, because he had walked the road and because that was who he was. He was a leader. All of it was new for me—i had never been there, never had those conversations. i ended up writing about it, two and a half pages with a title taken from a phrase inside the story. "To Write Love on Her Arms." Renee entered treatment and the story took on a life of its own. Messages arrived from around the world and curious t-shirts began showing up on stages and in airports and classrooms. Perhaps the rest is history, and i am thankful for that history.

But it goes back to David. He was the unsung hero. He was the quiet strength, the giant heart. He was the leader because he knew Renee's pain and he understood her disease, for it lived inside of him as well. She was a thing of contrast and he was absolutely that as well. Pain and hope, past and future, addiction and recovery, lies and truth, fears and dreams—they lived side by side inside him. Inside of both of them.

As the years went on, our friendship was challenged. David managed Renee, because she trusted him and because he knew business. And there was not a handbook for what was happening—how to navigate attention and money and mistakes and sobriety and privacy all mixed together. i was painted the hero as TWLOHA took off. There were highs and lows, arguments and lawyers and entire years of silence. Mostly there was distance.

Around 2009, i began hearing talk of a movie based on Renee's life, a story that would of course involve TWLOHA. David was the driving force behind it. People asked if i would be involved, if TWLOHA would be involved. Honestly, i was afraid and i was against it. How can we make a movie when we can't even be in the same room together? In the story they wanted to tell, was i the hero or the villain?

Months went by and my friend Cole e-mailed me to say the whole thing broke his heart. His e-mail broke the silence i had chosen. i didn't know how to deal with the situation so i simply avoided it. Cole said he wished for peace, that we could all be friends again. He said the movie shouldn't happen without me. i connected with his words, i wanted the same, but i didn't know how to get there. i ran into my friend Josh a couple of weeks later in Atlanta. Josh was involved in the movie and we ended up talking for five hours. By the end of the conversation, i felt hope that things could be restored.

i took a meeting with the movie folks and i ended up getting involved in the film. i said yes for two reasons:

1. i believed in the story. Believed it had the power to move people and so i cared how it was told.
2. i wanted my friends back. i wanted peace between us.

The movie was filmed over five weeks in Orlando in 2011. It was awkward walking onto the set the first day, but David and i quickly hugged and found a way to laugh. i was supposed to be on set for one day before leaving for Australia, but after a couple of hours on set, i knew that it was too special to walk away from. i canceled my Australia trip.

In the weeks that followed, David and i talked about the hard stuff. We apologized and said we loved each other. We started over. We started laughing again. We started rooting for each other again. i got my friend back.

There has been peace ever since. i wish we had spent more time together, but i am thankful that the pain gave way to peace. i knew that he loved me and he knew that i loved him. We were for the other, not against. i saw him a few times, mostly when we would bring staff and interns to his house to screen (see) the movie. He was always warm and kind, a gracious, generous host. We always made each other laugh. We talked about getting together, crossing the hour between us for we knew the friendship was more than worth the drive. But we were both busy and so it was always put on hold.

The last time i heard from David was on November 24. He reached out to tell me that he was touched by my Thanksgiving blog. We traded e-mails and agreed that we should get together soon. The last thing he said to me was that he loved me.

David was killed in a car accident two days ago. He was driving fast and it was late and i don't know the details. i don't know about his death but i know a few things about his life:

David McKenna was one of a kind. No part of him was average. He was passionate and generous and kind. i have never had more conflict with a person and yet it's hard to imagine liking a person more. We had a unique connection when it came to humor. i have so many memories of laughing so hard with David. He felt things deeply, believed deeply, worked hard. To have him in your corner was a powerful thing.

When i was first getting to know David, he invited me to the Grammys in Los Angeles. i was part of a group of seven or eight from Orlando, all David's friends. We had no business being there and knew nothing of how it worked. We just knew it was cool and that David had tickets and he wanted us there. i remember we were all super excited about the red carpet. We just assumed that if you went to the Grammys, you walked in with the stars. We learned that's not how it works, but that's not to say the night was a letdown. It's a memory i'm sure every one of those guys treasures today. i know i do.

When i was his roommate, our living room wasn't big but we had stadium seating and it's possible that the speakers were worth more than the house. He loved nice things. He loved film and music and the business of those worlds. He loved sharing things.

i wish we had another thirty years. i laugh through tears at the thought of him as an old man. He would have been a hilarious grumpy old man. Life is fragile and death is real and so we will not get to know. It's easy to ache for what's gone and for all that will not be. My heart breaks for his girlfriend, Andrea—

such a gift of beauty and grace, such a quiet strength in his life these last few years. My heart breaks for his parents and his brother and for his many friends. But, through these tears and through this ache a third straight day, i am also thankful.

i am thankful that i got to know David McKenna. i am thankful to be able to say that he is one of my all-time best friends. That i was known and loved by David is one of the great gifts of my life. i can hear his laughter, can hear his deep "That's awwwwwesome" and "Really, man? Really?" and "How are you?" We get a lot of how-are-you's in this life and they come in different shades. For me, David's was real and deep. We were both broken people and we knew it. We were both roller coasters. We both wore our hearts on our sleeves. We both believed big things were possible.

To Write Love on Her Arms would not exist if not for David McKenna. He didn't just provide the setting. Our story grew from his, from his war with addiction, from his fight for hope and change, for healing and sobriety.

And so this will be his legacy. Not all of it but part of it. This work we do, this message making its way around the world, this belief that healing can happen and that sobriety is worth fighting for, we will do this work for him.

When i stand onstage every night for three weeks on the HEAVY AND LIGHT tour, he will be inside me. i will remember his dreams and i will tell his story and i will cry for as long as it takes, for he is worth my tears. i will miss him backstage and in the balcony in Orlando on the last night of the tour. He spoke there last year. He and Renee shared and introduced a clip from the movie. He told me he was honored, that it meant the world to him to be included, to get to stand on stage.

If you love somebody, tell them. If there is conflict, let it go and fight instead for peace. Break the numb false silence and break the distance too. Laugh and cry and apologize and start again. This life is short and fragile but friendship is among the greatest miracles.

David McKenna was my friend. He changed my life. He loved me and i loved him and i will not forget him.

WONDERLAND & AFTER

(2013–2014)

BETWEEN TWO SEASONS

David Kuo was humble and wise, hilarious and kind. He was sensitive, emotional, intentional, and deep. He asked great questions. He asked the best questions. He was never in a hurry.

i had the privilege of knowing David for the last three years of his life. Cancer was either a reality or a possibility the entire time. And yet, when it came to our friendship, he was not the sick one and me the healthy. We both had our aching places. Mine could be called depression. My 2011 began with deep sadness—a broken heart after the sudden end of a relationship. i called David crying and he offered nothing small, nothing cheap or leading. He took a deep breath and said, "Oh, buddy. i'm so sorry. What a tragedy."

David started another round of radiation that week. And then on that Friday, after his fifth day of treatment, he boarded a plane to come to Florida. He didn't want me to be alone.

We sat on the beach, we watched movies, we ate good food,

we fed manatees—David adored manatees and i happen to live in manatee mecca. We listened to U2 and Michael Jackson and we talked for hours. In those hours i felt invited to be honest; i never had to fake it around David. We always found a way to laugh—with David, the laughter came easily.

There were other trips—two to Las Vegas. i watched him eat sushi at his favorite place and he spent most of that meal with his eyes closed. Words were replaced by groans of appreciation. He had a gift like that. He was excellent at wonder.

i never had a solution to his cancer. i could never promise healing. When healing would seem to settle in for a season, i could never promise it would stay. It was all a mystery to me. i didn't have answers but i learned the privilege of meeting my friend in his questions. And he seemed to do the same with me. With presence and laughter and sometimes words, we reminded the other that he did not walk alone. With David, i was invited to know him and to love him. And what a gift to have those things returned—to be known and loved by this extraordinary man.

We break in different ways in this life, all of us eventually. Perhaps we were made for heaven. i can begin to accept that, but i can't explain the suffering here. i don't have answers to the questions that come with good men leaving when it seems there was so much life still to live, so many people loving them and needing them.

Though i find comfort in the thought of my friend no longer suffering—he leaves much pain behind. David's playful youngest son will start kindergarten in the fall. His bright daughter is only 8 years old. His amazing best friend, Kim, is now a widow.

i don't know a lot but i've come to believe the following:

The world is broken. Our bodies break eventually. Our minds and hearts can break as well. We lose things in this life. We lose relationships. We lose people. And so a lot of folks live with a lot of pain. Much is mystery but God asks us to love, not just when it's easy and not just when a certain Scripture fits. What does it look like to love someone who lives in a place you've never been? When there are no words? Or what about allowing someone to love you when you feel completely alone, like no one can relate?

Beyond that, maybe it's better not to fake it, not to offer something cheap. For the rest of us still here, with air in our lungs and tears in our eyes, perhaps we are meant to simply meet one another in the questions. Though the price will be the heartache of loss—for we can't control when or how an ending comes—what a privilege that God allows us to connect with other people in this life, to be known and to be loved so we do not walk alone. Perhaps friendship—the deep kind, the best kind—perhaps it is a miracle.

My friend David lived that way. He lived a deep, intentional life. He listened and asked the best questions. He saw things and he said things and it made me feel like a million bucks, like maybe life could be rich, like maybe i was something good. David walked with dignity and grace in the face of enormous uncertainty. His cancer couldn't make him bitter, couldn't make him selfish. He asked great questions and he met me inside mine.

David Kuo gave me permission to be honest, permission to be me. He battled cancer and i battled depression and we could not fix each other. But what a gift to find a friend. What a gift for each of us—to get outside our heads and to see beyond our pain, to remind each other there was more to our stories. We were not simply broken things. He wasn't only Cancer and i wasn't only Sadness. And of course we had the bigger story too, the one that unites us, the one that finds richness and wonder in this life, and in the hope of heaven.

Last summer, in a Las Vegas hotel room (okay, it was a suite), in the presence of ten of his closest friends, David said this: "We will bury each other. If we get this right, it means we live life together and we love each other and we walk together. And in the end, one by one, we go home."

i spent my Easter at a hospice house in Charlotte, with David and his family. As i drove to the airport that afternoon, there was a stretch where, on my right, the trees along the road held not a single leaf. On my left, a perfect row of dogwoods stood covered in white, their full blooms declaring spring. It was a picture that echoed the day, an Easter spent between two seasons—between life and death, heaven and earth—but something in me has to believe the dogwoods win in the end.

WHERE IS THE WIND?

My mom just e-mailed me this photo. With her new iPhone, which she's figuring out, which makes me smile.

i'm headed west. Typing in the sky on the anniversary of the day the world stopped spinning, the day we were reminded that there is good and there is evil, there is love and there is hate. And life is fragile. Life is oh so short and fragile.

What do you love?

What would you die for?

What will you live for?

All my lists are getting shorter.

i spent the last three mornings with my nephew Landon in Florida. Today it was watermelon and toast and eggs but he didn't really like the eggs. He laughs now. He laughs so much. And it makes me laugh and it makes me smile. And those are things that have not always come easy and perhaps you can relate. He makes me smile and he makes me want to sit still and he causes me to notice things like birds and trees and wind. We go outside and i always ask him lately, "Where is the wind?" And of course there is no answer. The question doesn't even make sense but i like it for some reason.

Guess i'm saying that i feel it. That i notice. That it's there. Guess i'm saying i'm alive. Guess i'm saying thank you.

KUORVER

i had the privilege of introducing David Kuo to Kyle Korver a
couple of years back. Kyle was and is a professional athlete.
He plays in the NBA. David was a gifted writer who worked

in the White House and went on to write books. He was now fighting brain cancer, and had been for nearly a decade.

i had already made plans to have lunch with David in Charlotte when i found out Kyle was in town for a game. i told David that the three of us should have lunch. He was not happy. "I don't want to meet your NBA friend," he said. "I'm not impressed by that. And I got my daughter out of school to see you." i told David that his daughter was welcome to come to lunch—i had no reason to believe that Kyle hated children. This was classic David: sensitive, emotional, honest. David kicked and screamed but came to lunch and of course they had a great conversation and became fast friends.

The three of us would go to Vegas together, and New York. David stayed with Kyle in California and Kyle visited him in North Carolina. The three of us became something of a trio, something real and deep, fueled by David's questions and encouragement. We laughed a lot as well, and we ate sushi like it was going out of style.

Last year, Kyle gave David a jersey exactly like the one he wears in NBA games. The only difference was that Kyle added a U to his last name so that it began "KUO"—David's last name. The idea was actually mine, and i thought it was the coolest thing in the world.

David died in April. He was absolutely one of a kind. In some ways, he was the best friend i've ever had. He was the most encouraging voice in my life, and he taught me so much about love and honesty and friendship. Tonight, after the game in Orlando, Kyle handed me this jersey. There isn't much "stuff" at my house, and there isn't much "stuff" that i care about, but i will treasure this until the day i die.

EMPTY SEATS AT THE OSCARS

There were five nominees for Best Actor at the 2006 Oscars. We are without two of them tonight. Heath Ledger died in 2008, and Philip Seymour Hoffman died today, both brilliant artists gone too soon, both fathers and sons and brothers and friends, both lives taken by drug overdoses. If you want to look closer, Joaquin Phoenix lost his brother River to a drug overdose in 1993. Beyond that, Joaquin was nominated for his role in *Walk the Line*. He played Johnny Cash, the musical legend who, in real life, struggled for many years with drug addiction.

These famous names represent millions less known, millions of stories cut short, families with so much forever missing. Children shouldn't grow up without parents, and parents shouldn't have to bury their children.

This is what i've come to believe: There is much at stake. There are lives in the balance and ripples that push on for decades. Addiction is an awful beast to beat. It's never easy and it's never over and it will be a fight renewed each morning. But it's possible. i think of my uncle and my buddy Denny and so many people i've met on the road over the last eight years. Their lives are undeniable evidence that it's possible to change, that it's worth it to try and to keep trying, worth it to fight and keep fighting. Because this life is worth living. Because you are loved and made to be loved and made to give love and to experience a thousand wonderful things.

We're all in this together. It's okay to be honest. It's okay to ask for help. It's okay to say you're stuck, or that you're haunted or that you can't begin to let go. We can all relate to those things. Screw the stigma that says otherwise. Break the silence and break the cycle, for you are more than just your pain. You are not alone. And people need other people.

THROW THE ROCKS INTO THE INLET

Sometimes you have to travel far to find your heart. It may require airplanes and customs and multiple boat rides. Your phone won't work but after 24 hours you will be incredibly thankful for that. You will feel like a person again. You will remember that other people exist. You will remember your heart. You will cry more in three days than in the year leading up to the three days. The beauty of the place will be outdone only by the beauty of the conversations, by that miracle thing community. You will leave with new friends and perhaps a new heart. Throw the rocks into the inlet and cry for what's gone and what's missing but cry more for the beauty of what's there, the small army silent behind you, their patient presence saying, "We feel it too. We're broken too. We're all in this together." #LodgeFamily

MEET DREE

You land in Los Angeles. You are here to finish this book. You arrive sleepy, after a short morning flight from Tucson. You decide quickly that this morning will require a second cup of coffee. Which is perfect because there is a Starbucks next to the baggage claim. You are dressed head to toe in black, and you take your place in line, behind a girl dressed head to toe in white. She's pretty. White sweater, white jeans, white Converse. Her shoes are old. Pretty girls don't have to try. You like her shoes. She puts sunglasses on, black Ray-Bans, which is at least somewhat unusual because she is inside and the sun is outside. You wonder if perhaps it's because she doesn't want you to look at her.

At this point, you wish to speak to her. But of course you can't because what would you say? And it's the worst to be unwelcome. She takes her sunglasses off. She presses the Uber button on her phone and suddenly it hits you—you're about to do the exact same thing. And because you are uncertain of how the process works, you have a reasonable question to ask this woman. So you tap her on the shoulder. She turns and looks at you and oh-my-God-she's-gorgeous. She is impossibly beautiful. Those light eyes.

You talk about Uber.

She's not from here.

Where is she from?

She's from New York.

You used to live in New York. Fourteenth and Third.

She lives in the West Village.

You guess that she's a model.

She adds that she's an actress. Her name is Dree. Her mom lives in Malibu.

You love the corn at Café Habana in Malibu.

She agrees. She's originally from Idaho.

You've been to Boise. You've been everywhere.

She starts to say goodbye but you both have to walk to baggage claim. So you keep talking. You have completely forgotten about the Uber button you had planned to press. You have turned into a puppy, because this is who you are and this is how you're wired. You feel too much. And she looks like your biggest dream, the one where you get to share your heart and share your life, the one where you come home to someone beautiful.

She picks up her bag. Black Patagonia. Waterproof. Perhaps she's a surfer. You have met the perfect girl.

You walk to the curb. Her car arrives. A black SUV. (You have still yet to request yours.) Moment of truth. You ask for her number or it's goodbye forever.

"Can we be friends or do you have enough friends?" (Holy shit, you were brave.)

She laughs.

"Yes, we can be friends."

You pull out your phone and you say that you will text her.

She speaks her number and you type her number.

You send the word "Hello."

The driver loads her bags and then he starts to load your bags. You stop him. You both laugh. You hug.

She gets in and the car drives away and she waves while it does.

She texts you instantly. "Amazing."

Your car arrives a few minutes later. A white Prius. You text back, "She wore white and got into a black SUV. He wore black and got into a white Prius. They headed off in the directions of their separate special canyons."

You're a writer.

You are old-fashioned so of course you Google her instantly, curious to know more about the mysterious beautiful creature you just met.

You type in "Dree model," wondering if that will be enough to find her.

Dree Hemingway. She is the great-granddaughter of the writer Ernest Hemingway.

If a man can't finish a book after randomly meeting the beautiful great-granddaughter of Ernest Hemingway, then a man can't finish a book.

HOLDING ON AND LETTING GO

Isaiah Austin was supposed to get drafted tonight. He was supposed to become a millionaire. His entire life was leading up to this moment. The thousands of hours dominating on the basketball court—as a kid, in high school, in college. And then a few days ago, he was told he can't play basketball anymore, because something is wrong inside his body. It's not his fault, it can't be fixed, it's beyond his control.

And just like that, his basketball career is over.

Isaiah has handled the whole thing with impossible positivity and poise and grace, saying he will learn to dream new dreams, saying he is grateful for all the years of basketball and all it gave him.

And then tonight, this moment.

The NBA wanted him to have the experience of getting drafted. In the middle of the first round, they called his name. Standing ovation. The same walk to the stage as all the other players, the same photo moment with the commissioner.

And it hit me: This appeared a victory but it was literally a loss. They let him experience the thing being taken. "You can taste this, but you will never have this."

And something else hit me: What a powerful thing to love someone as they lose, to stand and clap and cry, simply to express, "We see you. We're so beyond sorry. You matter. Your pain matters. The death of your dream matters. You are not alone in this moment." And what a powerful thing to watch someone lose with grace, to watch someone hold on and let go all at once. We are meant to win and lose together.

i'll leave you with something i heard at lunch today: "Life's basically about these two questions: What will you celebrate? What will you grieve?"

DREAMS TO KEEP DREAMING

My parents lost a baby boy thirty-seven years ago today. Doctors told them to stop trying to have kids. i'm glad they didn't listen.

My brother was born and died the same day. My Mom and Dad gave him a name and i suppose they did that to say that he had lived, to say that he mattered, and to say they would remember. My brother's name was Jesse.

My parents went on to have me, and then three years later my sister Jessica, and six years after that, my sister Emily. Jessica and her husband, Sean, tried for three years to get pregnant. They eventually decided to do IVF and posted a blog inviting people to donate to help pay for the expensive procedure. Friends and family and even strangers gave more than $10,000. When my nephew Landon was born, the *New York Times* called him "the world's first crowd-funded baby." Two years later, Jessica got pregnant again, this time a total surprise. i remember finding out and crying because the news seemed impossible. Jess jokes it was "buy one, get one free." Declan is here and healthy and getting bigger every day.

The moral of the story: It seems to me that much of life is figuring out what to hold on to and what to let go of. i know there are some dreams we have to eventually release, but there are also dreams to keep dreaming. Tonight i'm glad my mom didn't give up on her dream of having children. And that years later, her courage and strength would inspire her daughter to do the very same thing.

(In other news, i'm told that Landon peed in the toilet today. He mostly missed but hey, you gotta start somewhere.)

JASON RUSSELL PART 2

We don't talk all that much. We mostly text. Lots of jokes. But there's a bond. There's an understanding. His lowest moment was a very public thing. And in that moment, i did not feel far from him. In that moment, i felt the same as him. The edge is not so far. We break in different ways. i know what it is to be called the hero, and i've heard "villain" too. Both have a way of messing with you. One of the proudest moments of my life came in the minutes after Jason's breakdown. As the world started to speculate and guess, as the ugly jokes began to fly, i sat alone in a coffee shop on Larchmont Boulevard in Los Angeles. i wrote a blog called "Jason Russell is my friend." i didn't know the whole story, didn't know the details of what happened. In a way, it didn't matter. i just wanted my friend to be okay. Jason went away. He got help. He took a break. He is doing great today. And the story goes like this: 150 people were invited to the White House last summer—150 leaders who work in mental health. i may have been the only one who asked to bring a friend. The President spoke. And it was my great honor to show up with this guy. Jason Russell is my friend. And a friend is no small thing.

THERE IS STILL SOME TIME

If you feel too much, there's still a place for you
 here.
If you feel too much, don't go.
If this world is too painful, stop and rest.
It's okay to stop and rest.
If you need a break, it's okay to say you need a
 break.
This life—it's not a contest, not a race, not a
 performance, not a thing that you win.
It's okay to slow down.
You are here for more than grades, more than a
 job, more than a promotion, more than keeping
 up, more than getting by.
This life is not about status or opinion or
 appearance.
You don't have to fake it.
You do not have to fake it.
Other people feel this way too.

If your heart is broken, it's okay to say your heart is broken.

If you feel stuck, it's okay to say you feel stuck.

If you can't let go, it's okay to say you can't let go.

You are not alone in these places.

Other people feel how you feel.

You are more than just your pain. You are more than wounds, more than drugs, more than death and silence.

There is still some time to be surprised.

There is still some time to ask for help.

There is still some time to start again.

There is still some time for love to find you.

It's not too late.

You're not alone.

It's okay—whatever you need and however long it takes—it's okay.

It's okay.

If you feel too much, there's still a place for you here.

If you feel too much, don't go.

There is still some time.

DISCLAIMER

This brings us to the end of our journey. It means the world that you've chosen to sit with all these stories. But there's something more i have to tell you. It's a bit of a disclaimer, which i know is odd because disclaimers usually come at the beginning. The disclaimer is this: My goal is not to impress you with my stories or the stories of my friends. My goal is not to make you think i'm a good writer. i want to shift the focus, to redirect the lights. i want to focus on your story. i don't know if you've ever thought of it that way—that metaphor, that idea, your life as a story—but let's see what we can find there.

If it's true that you and i are living stories, then isn't it true that there are parts of our stories we don't like? Perhaps there are parts of our stories that we even hate. There are moments we feel stuck in, things we wish we could forget, pages and paragraphs—even entire chapters—we wish we could remove. And the longer we live, the further we get down these roads, the harder it is to live in the present. Because we lose things—

we lose people, we lose relationships—and we are tempted to go back. We reach for the past. We try to press rewind.

And then somehow, within the same story of your life, there are things you love. Things that make you laugh and make you smile. There are relationships and moments and conversations—favorite people, favorite places, favorite days. There are favorite books and films and songs—the way they speak to you and remind you you're alive. A case can be made that you are early in your story, still so many pages left to write and read. Consider your dreams. Perhaps it's a career you hope to achieve, something you feel born to fix or build. Maybe it's a place you hope to live or simply visit. Maybe it's the idea of having a family, of being a mother or a father, a husband or a wife.

What if all those things that make up your story, the hard stuff and the good stuff, all the fears and dreams—what if all of it matters? i want to suggest the possibility that right now, today, tonight, you are living a story that is entirely unique, a story that is sacred and priceless, one where no one else can play your part. My poet friend Sierra has a poem, and this poem suggests that your voice is someone's favorite voice, your face is someone's favorite face. i hope those words feel true.

And my hope is that you won't just take her word for it, or my word for it. You deserve better. You deserve more. It seems to me that every good story requires more than one character—two people or a few people walking through something together, overcoming something together. It's never just one person. And so i wonder if you have that? Do you have those other characters? Those folks who you can lean on, the people you can call in the middle of the night, people who know you and love you, relationships where those things are exchanged. If you don't have it, do you believe that you deserve it?

And should you ever get to a place where you consider giving up on your story, if the pain feels like too much to bear, i pray those people will step in and remind you just how much you matter, that your story is worth fighting for. Whether it's with their words or with their presence, may they meet you in those hardest moments, to say you're not alone, to say your story is also theirs, and that theirs is yours as well. i hope you have those friends, and i hope you get to be that sort of friend.

More than anything, my wish for you is this: That when your awful darkest days come, you will know you're not alone. Pain will tell you to keep quiet, but that's a lie. Life is fragile and we all break in different ways. i hope you know you can be honest. i hope you know that you can ask for help. Did you catch that? It is absolutely positively okay to ask for help. It simply means you're human. Help is real and it is possible; people find it every day.

Many live alone on islands made of nightmares. May we live as boats and bridges sent through darkness, honest boats and bridges sent to find them. May we build those things, and may we also be them. And may we raise an honest hand on days we need them. And then, after help and rest and all the things our lives require, let's keep going. There is still so much to feel and see and say.

HEART CAMP

(2015–2016)

TO THE GUY IN 15F

"Be kind, for everyone you meet is fighting a hard battle."
—Source Unknown

This was true of Aaron Carter last night, but few people were kind.

Ten years ago, Aaron was a teenage pop star. That's what most people remember, but it's been years since Aaron had a hit song or made headlines with good news. Last night, he tweeted about struggling with his weight, about dealing with anxiety. And then the Internet went wild when he "compared himself to Michael Jackson." Aaron was an easy target, his words misunderstood.

We forget that famous people are real people with real problems and real feelings. We forget that the things we say online can have real consequences. And why is it that we love to watch someone fall?

i had an unusual perspective last night, and i don't mean because i work in mental health. i mean that as Aaron tweeted from seat 15F on that Delta flight from Orlando to LA, i was about five feet away, seated in 13C.

i first noticed him as we boarded the flight, a young man on the phone and clearly having a hard time. i recognized him but couldn't place him and then it hit me: "i think that's Aaron Carter." i googled the name and sure enough, the photos matched the guy two rows behind me. i looked at his Twitter and it was clear that the hard time was not confined to one phone call. His Twitter was a sea of confessions and explanations and trying to defend himself from people being mean.

i tweeted to him, "i'm on your flight, in row 13 if you need someone to talk to. Peace to You."

No response. i watched as the tweets continued. i kept looking back to see him staring at his phone, typing constantly. And in that moment, i recognized him. And i'm not talking about fame, i mean i've been there and maybe you've been there as well. Not with half a million followers and not with our tweets making headlines. But i know that feeling of fighting to explain and to defend, using words in hoping to be understood, but then it ends up going south.

i knew he couldn't win. His words were only fueling the fire, only giving the haters more material. The whole thing made me sad. i pulled a notebook and a Sharpie from my backpack and started to write: "i'm sorry for the hate on Twitter. People love to hate. i'm here if you want to talk." i stood up, took three steps in his direction, and handed him the piece of paper. He thanked me. A few minutes later, he tapped me on the shoulder and we walked to the back of the plane.

We talked for about ten minutes. We got cut short by the flight attendants who seemed excited to be talking to a famous person. We didn't get to trade info. i didn't make an epic speech. i'm not the hero in this story.

By the time we landed, Aaron's tweets had made their way to Cosmo and E! and Perez Hilton. People were using words like "meltdown" and "rant." My own friends, people i follow and respect, were adding to the noise.

There's something i wanted to say to Aaron last night, but i didn't get the chance. i would like to share it here:

You don't have to convince anyone. Your value is not based on performance. You deserve love. You deserve friends. You're enough.

People found his Michael Jackson tweet hilarious. Aaron said that Michael had once passed the torch to him. People took it as if the words were Aaron's, but really, he was sharing a story from his youth. As a young superstar, Aaron got to know Michael Jackson and Michael had told him he was next.

Michael Jackson is perhaps the most legendary singer of all time, in a league of his own. Aaron's career peaked when he was a teenager. He has not released new music in ten years. People were quick and mean in pointing out the space between the two performers.

The MJ story stayed with me. i wondered why he chose to share it, what might be at the heart of it. i didn't get to ask him so this is only my opinion but i feel like it's worth sharing. i wonder if that story, the one that made headlines from the fifteenth row of a cross-country flight last night, the one so many people twisted and used against Aaron, i wonder if there's another way to translate it.

Here's what i think Aaron Carter was trying to communicate: "Someone great believed in me once. It felt really good. It meant a lot to me. My story isn't over. My career isn't over. I'm still alive and I remember Michael's words because there's hope inside those words. And in a difficult moment, hope is no small thing."

Aaron Carter is a real person. He may not be "the next Michael Jackson" but that isn't the point. He is a brother and a son, a person who no doubt has lived a very unique life, amazing in ways but challenging as well. And at twenty-seven, i hope he's early in his story. This book exists to say that every person matters, every life and every story. Aaron Carter is included.

So to the guy in 15F:

i'm sorry for the hate. Please know you're not alone. You don't owe the haters anything. Whether you go on to release the greatest album of all time or never write another song, you matter infinitely. Your life is priceless. You deserve love. Not for any performance or success but simply because you're alive. And if you need someone to talk to, i'm in row 13.

Peace to You.
jamie

VANCOUVER

The photo on the cover of this book, it was taken in Vancouver. i remember wondering if it was weird to choose a photo of a place that wasn't central to my story, but the picture matched the vision in my head. It represented holidays and wonder, people together and people alone, some gathered to celebrate, others aware of things missing.

You were home when we were introduced, through a simple text message from a mutual friend. You were staying with your family for the holidays. i asked if we could talk for one minute and we talked for one hour. It would end up being one of our shorter conversations.

i sent you a copy of this book but you bought your own before it arrived. You said the pages made you cry, because you recognized my heart. You said the book was important because it allowed you to trust me, because the words were written long before we knew each other. It couldn't be me telling you what you wanted to hear because i had no way of knowing. You felt the words just might be true.

We talked and texted every day for hours, for a week before i went to Hawaii. We talked for hours while i was there. It's hard for my brain to process that you weren't physically with me in Hawaii, because you're in almost every memory. It was a joy to begin to share my life with you, to laugh and trade the stories of our days. My best friend Mark and i were staying together, and you and i were setting FaceTime world records, but Mark didn't mind because he knows my biggest dream.

i had a book event in Honolulu, an hour's drive from our hotel on the North Shore. You were with us the entire time. And we found a way to webcast the event, mostly so you could watch it. You watched the whole thing, and i remember calling from the restaurant right after. i have never enjoyed talking to someone more. You had my attention, and it meant the world that somehow i had yours. You so quickly felt like home.

My round trip tickets were booked before i knew you, but by this point, i knew i wouldn't be on the flight back to Florida. That said, i also knew that it was time for me to go. i realize most people wouldn't trade Hawaiian sand for northern snow but, to paraphrase Robin Williams in *Good Will Hunting*, i had to see about a girl.

i left Honolulu at night and i don't think i slept at all. My chest was Christmas morning. The plane landed in Vancouver just after sunrise. At Customs, an officer asked the purpose of my visit. i smiled and said that i was there to see a friend. He asked your name and i gave your name with pride.

Do you remember when we saw each other for the first time? i came through the doors and you were there among the crowd. We both smiled giant smiles. i walked those final steps and you kissed me the moment i arrived. Of course i hoped to kiss you, but i didn't know when it might happen. You were embarrassed and kept laughing and apologizing and i kept smiling because i was so happy to be kissing you.

We walked to your car and immediately i liked it. Dark and sleek and strong, humble and cool, in those ways like its owner. You didn't need a status symbol. You didn't need an announcement of your income. i was so happy to be stepping inside, to start to go together.

You handed me the token that we needed to pay for parking but i didn't realize what it was. In the thirty seconds from when you gave it to me to when you asked for it back, i somehow managed to lose it. You were baffled at how such a thing was even possible. You eventually found it and we could not stop laughing. And we laughed each time it was relived. You loved to tell that story and i loved to hear it told.

i spent four days with you in Vancouver. i met your parents and your sisters, and both of your best friends. One of those friends was covered in bright white fur and it meant a lot when you told me that you liked the way i treated her, that i was different from the men who came before me. We went to church to see your niece sing Christmas songs. You took me ice skating and we laughed at how terrible i was. (i smiled at how good you were.) We ballroom danced on the sidewalk on the way to the Italian restaurant downtown. We both loved that dinner. i wanted to buy a Canucks shirt but we were pressed for time. i wish that i had bought one. i loved that night. i loved my time with you in your city. i was five thousand miles from home but i felt so much at home.

i flew to Florida for Christmas and then back to Vancouver two weeks later, to be with you on your drive back to Los Angeles. We had breakfast with your parents and we picked up Thai food for everyone that night. After dinner, i went out with your sister's husband and your dad. A pub was not my normal scene but the occasion felt significant, like i was suddenly among new characters in my story, because these were important characters in your story.

Your dad spoke gently. He talked about the pain of the last year and i liked him very much. i wanted to be the season's hero, the thing that said those old broken days were simply gone.

You cried the next morning as we left your parents' house. You said it's always hard to say goodbye. i felt a sense of pride and responsibility. i felt honored to be next to you, excited for the journey ahead, and full of hope for all that we would build and share.

i would lose you five weeks later in Los Angeles. In your living room in Venice and on Valentine's Day. Perhaps it was too much too soon. Perhaps you got scared. There were cracks and old wounds and hard moments and i suppose it reminded you of other things that fell apart. i begged and hung on and leaked ten thousand words.

i haven't seen your face or heard your voice in more days than the number that i knew you. i feel embarrassed when people ask how long we dated, because i know the days don't match the weight of what i feel. But if a day can change your life, a lot can happen in sixty-eight of them. And it's hard to unknow your favorite person. It's hard to let go of what you love.

For what it's worth, i would do it all again. i would get on that plane today, to Vancouver or Los Angeles or absolutely anywhere. i type these words through eyes now filled with tears.

The place in the picture on the cover of this book, it isn't random anymore. i've been to Vancouver. i've danced on frozen streets and left town with precious cargo. i once declared your name.

As for the pages behind that evening sky, you were my favorite audience. When you said you saw my heart, when you said my heart was good, you made it all make sense. If this book was only written for you, that would be enough. And now a new edition and you're not in my life but you're in nearly every added word.

i suppose you found your way into the subtitle as well. Found and lost and hoped for.

i am lost but i hope one day to be found.

Thank you for the days you felt like home.

SORROW IS AN INJURY

"If your heart is broken, it's okay to say your heart is broken."

Those words show up a few pages back, in the same piece that inspired the title of this book. i read them out loud every single night on the book tour, and i shared them again last night, on a stage at Lindenwood University, just outside St. Louis.

i added another statement last night and that statement is true again today:

My heart is broken.

i don't want to talk a lot about it here. This isn't the place for it. But i do want to be honest about that fact, and mostly i want to share what's happened in the last few days, as i've been honest about my pain.

My friend Jon invited me to stay with him. He said stay as long as you need to. He said, "There is a rock at the beach and

I go there every night to pray. I've never shared it with anyone but I would be honored to share it with you." We went to the beach late that night and beneath a full moon and a sky full of stars, Jon prayed for me. The waves reflected all of it.

That same night, he sat with me, his arm around me while i cried. He did it again the following morning, when i was too sad to leave the house. He bought me lunch. When i left, he said, "Call me anytime day or night." He called me first thing the following morning, to ask how i was doing.

My friend Jason listened for a long time. He is happily married to his high school sweetheart and so it crossed my mind that he might not relate to heartache. i was proven wrong when he opened up about the last year, calling it the hardest of his life. It was not pain related to romance but the loss of his career and sense of purpose. He continues to wrestle with deep regret and questions about his identity.

My best friend Mark offered to fly to St. Louis, so that i would not have to do the speaking event by myself. He is busy and has a family and St. Louis on no notice was probably not at the top of his list, but he didn't hesitate. He didn't want me to be alone and so he offered to go with me.

Another friend texted: "I'm always available for you. Be good to your heart. These are tender days and don't let them break you."

Someone else wrote, "I'm so sorry to hear your heart is hurting. I love you. I'm with you. I will pray for you and I will check in on you this week. And if there is anything that you need, you let me know."

i was with my sisters two days ago in Los Angeles. Emily lives there and Jessica had flown across the country for a visit, my nephew Landon's first time on an airplane and first trip to California. We took Landon to the zoo. i was there but i wasn't. i was in my head. i could tell that Jess and Emily didn't know how to help me, didn't know what to do or say. They've seen me like this before, years ago. We went back to Emily's house and i asked both of them to sit with me. i was honest about my pain. They asked questions and listened and offered advice. Jess said she's never seen a person fall so hard. i cried a lot but it felt good to get it out.

Yesterday i flew to St. Louis for the Lindenwood event. My friend Steven joined me to play music, as he often does. After the event, as i was wondering if i had shared too much, if my words had made any sense, the sound engineer knocked on the door of the greenroom. "I didn't know anything about this event when I got here today. I thought I was just coming to work. But I want to thank you because it spoke to my soul." We talked for a few minutes about the common ground between our stories, his recent breakup and the pain he has survived.

The school booked Steven and me two hotel rooms last night, but i asked him if we could just share one room instead.

i didn't want to be alone. When i got out of the shower, the TV was on and i asked Steven if we could turn it off. i wanted to talk. i wanted his advice. He listened and he talked about his own struggles, his own questions and recent breakthroughs. He encouraged me, told me what he sees in me.

i had a return ticket to fly back to Los Angeles the very next day but things were different now. LA would be too painful. It was time to head home to Florida, time to grieve and slowly, eventually, start to heal.

It's been a hard week, but i can't imagine how much harder it would have been without the love of my friends and family. i have survived on their support and wisdom and comfort. And the key was that i had to tell them. i had to be honest about my pain, had to choose to let them in, and choose to let them love me.

i woke up early today and flew back to Florida and now i'm home. i live alone and it's quiet. My phone is not ringing and that has been the hardest thing. My phone reminds me of her. So many things remind me of her. But it's just me right now. Today has been a hard day. My heart is heavy. My life looks different than it did a few days ago.

How will i feel tonight?

i don't know.

How will i feel tomorrow?

i don't know.

How will i feel next week?

i don't know.

But i know i need to keep being honest. About where i'm at and what i need and what i can and can't handle. i know i need to talk sometimes and cry sometimes and also be quiet sometimes. i need to play with my nephews and i need to eat and sleep and exercise.

i just made an appointment to go back to counseling. It's one thing to tell people that it's good to go to counseling. It's another thing to take my own advice.

If your heart is broken, it's okay to say your heart is broken.

Sorrow is an injury. This is going to take some time. Please be gentle with yourself.

IF HE SAID IT LOUD ENOUGH

My nephew Landon said your name last night. We were on FaceTime and he asked if he could tell you his joke, the one he always told you, the one where he starts laughing the second that he finishes. i always loved the exchange, him talking so fast and then both of you laughing. i loved watching you get to know my family and i loved watching them get to know you. i wish that you had come to Florida.

It's been weeks without him seeing you and no one said your name, so i don't know what made him think of you. i suppose it was FaceTime. Talking to me must have reminded him of talking to you.

Landon asked Jess if he could tell you the joke. He said that if he said it loud enough, maybe you would hear him.

i tried not to cry.

Everything in me wished he could be right. i wish it worked that way. i wish that you could hear him, and laugh with us again. i wish that i could see and hear you, and i hope God hears all my prayers.

NOTE TO SELF (BE STILL)

i know you don't know how to do this. i know the silence feels impossible. i know the weight you feel most mornings, even this morning, even now.

i know how much you miss her, miss her friendship most of all. i know how much you loved the conversations.

i know how excited you were, how much you believed. i know the dreams you started dreaming.

i know you wanted to frame and hang those photographs. i know you love the one from Big Sur that looks borrowed from a fairy tale; she is strong there standing staring at the ocean, her beauty mixed with all the beauty of the place. And the photo from the car the day before—she's kissing your cheek and you're smiling ear to ear. i remember the pride you felt as you drove through the nasty weather, on the 5 south out of Oregon. You had to keep her safe. You had to get her home. The whole thing felt important.

Those photographs were moments that you cherished and you captured. They've been deleted but you don't know how to let them go. i know so much of you is holding on. Of course i know you still believe. i know this note is also a time capsule, a message in a bottle you hope might wash up on her shore. i know you dream she might remember, feel the things she felt and see the things she saw.

i know the hard moments aren't what haunts you. It's not the days you argued, not the day she said good-bye. You're haunted by the good days, the great days, and the way they disappeared. What do you do now with those memories, with all those hours on the phone, "good morning" texts that made you smile, every inside joke? You were getting to know this extraordinary person and it brought you so much joy. i know the meaning that you found in so many simple moments—making dinner in her kitchen, discovering she was better than you at basketball. i know what it meant to be with her on your birthday, the feeling that your life was no longer just your own. i know how much it meant to see her get to know your sisters. i know that you were falling in love and i know you don't know what to do with any of this now.

You told Hank you keep going over the whole thing in your head. You were walking with her and then suddenly she was gone. You can't make any sense of it. He said of course it doesn't make sense. Perhaps it actually has very little to do with you. She just wasn't ready. She got scared and ran away.

And i know you would give anything to go with her, to walk with her again, to fight away the ghosts and lies of the men who came before you. i know you wish you could remind her of what's true, that her dreams can all be dreamed again, that things can be made new. i know you keep going back to ideas that you two talked about, choosing love over fear, and the quote from The Shack, that healing can arrive in the same manner as the wound—we get hurt in relationships, but God can use them also to restore.

i know everything in you still believes the thing you said to her: "It's just us. It's you and me. We can do this. We can figure this out together." But she chose to go alone. And i know it's the hardest thing in the world, but to love her now means to honor her decision, to let her walk away. You speak right now with silence, and with the prayers you pray each night.

i know you question the motives of "Heart Camp", which is what you're calling life these days. Because she inspired all the changes you've been making. She asked why you had to always go to Starbucks, and why your walls were empty. Now there's a coffeemaker in your kitchen, and framed posters in your living room. i know you wish that she could see them. You sit and read lately, every single morning at the beach you used to take for granted. You've been using your mind again, and opening your heart. You're looking for God and asking God to look for you. You've been praying for a long time before you go to sleep, prayers of desperation and surrender, prayers of letting go but also holding on.

Your skin is tan from surfing. You've done it five days

straight. Your chest is sore from push-ups, and you feel the running in your legs. You can see and feel your body getting stronger, and you wish that she could see it too. You were numb and lazy for a long time, and your faith became so tangled. You are so much more alive now. This, you, now, it's everything she hoped for you. And so of course you wonder if it's ridiculous to keep doing all these things. She was the spark but she's no longer in your life. Well, i hope that you keep going. Because all these things are good for you, and all these things are you. Hear that again: None of this is new inside your life. It's just you coming home. Keep walking with God. Keep reading every day. Keep surfing because surfing is a big part of who you are, since you were a little boy. You joke that it's like free counseling because you like yourself more right after. (Keep going to actual counseling as well.) i know that basketball is hard because it reminds you of her, so leave that be for now. But this stuff is you and this stuff is healthy, and you should be proud. This is living well. This is how it's meant to be.

i know you pray for her every single night, and you aren't sure if that's okay. You pray for her heart, for her healing, for her safety. i know you're doing your best to surrender, to trust God with all of it, with your pain, with hers, with your heart and with your dreams.

Keep being honest, with God, with your counselor, with

your parents and your sisters and your friends. i know it feels important to spend a lot of time alone right now, but don't forget to lean on people too. A lot of people love you. Don't forget to let them. They are so important to this process and to your life in general. They can see some things you can't right now. And please keep doing what you've been called to do, keep sharing from your journey. You can offer words of hope and love to people, even from this painful place. You've been doing it and you should keep doing it. That's the call placed on your life. It's your gift and your responsibility.

Continue to communicate. Continue to bring light to dark places, even as you struggle. Continue to hold the flag for love and hope. It's what you were made to do.

Avoid the broken questions. "Will she ever call?" and "What if she meets someone?" and "I'll never meet someone…" Don't go there. It's madness. You can't control those things and so much of that is fear. You don't have to live in fear.

You're going to get through this. The pain won't last forever. You will be loved and you will get to love again. So keep going, even if it's slowly. See what's around this corner. See where the road ends up ahead. If you get discouraged, think back upon your journey. You've tasted so much and known so many great surprises. Isn't it reasonable to think that more are on the way? Good things will find you once again.

You've been searching for a new song, for words that might

bring comfort and a place where you feel safe. You had forgotten about Isaac singing "Be Still" until yesterday. Since then, it's been on repeat, it is playing even now. Rest within the heartbeat of that piano, and the way these words feel true.

Be still.

ACKNOWLEDGMENTS

It was Bryan Norman whose *Jerry Maguire* e-mail set this book in motion. Before that e-mail, there was a conversation along the Princess Louisa Inlet in British Columbia. That conversation happened because of Bob Goff and Donald Miller, because of their desire for people to be known and loved. In addition to the friendships and the healing that i found along that inlet, i ended up with an agent. After years of dreaming about a book, Bryan was the push and spark that helped it happen.

James Likeness designed the cover of this book. He spent hours trying different ideas, going back and forth with me on iChat, willing to include me in the process, as he has for so many different projects over the years. i'm grateful to James for his patience and dedication. i love this cover and i love that we got to work on it together. Thanks for putting up with me.

So much of the writing in this book did not come easy. My parents and sisters are the ones who paid the price. i would show up late to family gatherings, or simply leave the room to write. i've never written consistently, so when it comes it comes. i suppose my experience with depression has been the same. i'm grateful to my family for their support through both, for encouraging me to write, and for wanting more than anything to see me smile.

To Sean Haley: Thanks for loving Jessica and Landon and Declan. And thanks for tolerating the many quirks and laughs of the family you inherited when you married Jess. i'm so glad you guys chose each other. We are lucky to have you.

To my nephews, Landon and Declan: Most of this book was written before you were born. Landon is two and almost three as i write this. Declan just turned one. Your arrival changed everything. i know no greater joy than when i get to see you smile. Landon, there was a night while this book was being made, when things were very hard. i started to cry and you said to me, "Don't cry, Uncle Jamie." You kept saying it and you said it in a way that made clear how much you loved me. You were only two but you were fighting for me. It was a moment i'll never forget.

Mark Codgen and Ian Soto have been my two best friends for more than twenty years. We've lived a thousand different stories. i couldn't ask for two better characters to join me on this journey.

Kyle Korver's kindness and humility are as hard to fathom as his jump shot, which is the best in the world. Thanks for rooting for me.

No one inspires me more than Jon Foreman. He writes and sings some of my favorite songs. Jon once told me that i needed to be careful with my heart, because my heart was filled with songs. He said that his songs, the kind with verse and chorus, they leave room to hide. Mine were simply me showing someone my heart, and so my heart required care. That conversation meant the world to me.

To Byron Cutrer: It's hard to find the words. You have taught me so much and you have been there for me. Thanks for allowing me to share part of your story in this book.

Josh Hartzler is the guy i call when i feel too much. Thanks for your encouragement and thank you for believing in me.

CJ and Damien Hobgood have been letting me tag along since we were in high school. Back then, the trips were to New Smyrna and Sebastian Inlet. A few years later, it was Hawaii and Australia and

France. i never stopped looking up to you guys. i've always been so proud to call you friends.

Bob Hurley gave me a huge job when i was twenty-two years old. i should have been two hundredth in line but there was no line, because Bob didn't even interview anyone else. Along with Paul Gomez, he saw something in me and took a chance on me, and it changed my life. i was grateful then and i was grateful four years later when he supported my decision to leave to start TWLOHA. Bob, thank you for your support, your wisdom, your enthusiasm. Thanks for inspiring me and thanks for being my friend.

It's hard to imagine the last ten years without Josh Loveless. Honestly, i can't.

Jason Russell is my friend. He gives me permission to be me.

To Jon Tyson: You're one of my heroes. i respect you so much.

Meeting Renee Yohe changed my life, and today i'm proud to be able to say that she's my friend. Thanks for your forgiveness and patience and grace.

TWLOHA would not have happened without the support of Switchfoot and Anberlin. i'll be thanking them for the rest of my life.

Right after i wrote the original TWLOHA story, Craig Gross invited me to come spend a month with him and his family. He had never met me but said that i should come live in his basement. i followed him around for a month, i asked a million questions, and we've been friends ever since.

Chris Heuertz is one of the wonders of the world. The guy is extraordinary and i am proud to know him.

My uncle John is a great storyteller, and he's living one of my favorite stories.

Kate and David Hodges have provided me with weeks and weeks of shelter in Los Angeles. More than that, they are my friends and David is evidence that doing great work does not depend on being awake at 9 AM.

To Dree Hemingway: Thanks for letting me write about you. i'm glad it made you smile.

If Nashville had an ocean, i would move there tomorrow. i would spend my time with Steven and Danielle McMorran, Don and Betsy Miller, Matt Wertz, Dave Barnes, Jeremy Cowart, Chris and Alyce Youngblood, Skip Matheny, Carlos Whitaker, Thad Cockrell, Chuck and Pap Shirock, and Cadence Turpin. (Cadence is the best name ever.) i would also hope to hang with Mat Kearney. The longest conversation that i've ever had with Mat was about the title of this book. i didn't go with his suggestion, but i like him very much.

When the U.S. Women's National Soccer Team takes the field for the World Cup, i'll be cheering for my friends. Those friendships exist because of Ashlyn Harris, who is in a league of her own when it comes to passion, loyalty, and generosity. The rest of the gang is Alex "Unicorns Are People Too" Morgan, Christen "National Coffee Day" Press, Ali Krieger, Whitney Engen, and Heather O'Reilly.

To my cousins: Walter, Liam, April, Joseph, Sarah, Megan, Charlie, Max, Chelsea, Spencer, Owen, Lisa, Johnny, Amy, Luke, Gemma, and Sarah: Here's to the kids table.

The friendship and encouragement of the following people contributed to this book: Gord Marriage, Danny Wheatley, Bob Rohmann, Gabe Lyons, Chase Reeves, Bryce & Tara Avary, Dustin Kensrue, John Sowers, Joel Houston, Tom Shadyac, John Campbell, Chad Butler, Tim Foreman, Drew Shirley, Tara & Eric Brown, Kelly Slater, Kyle Griner, Nate Young, Deon Rexroat, Stephen Christian, Denny & Lindsay Kolsch, Aaron & Michelle Moore, Chad Moses, Jason Blades, Lauren Gloyne, Joe Napier, Bryan Funk, Jonathan Frazier, Claire Biggs, Jim Hoyle, Rich Sullivan, Damion Suomi, Logan & Phillip Watters, Justin Purser, Jarrett Stevens, Anthony Raneri, Aaron Gillespie, Noah Gundersen, Roxanne Stone, Kevin Breel, Anis Mojgani, Sierra DeMulder, Dayna Ghiraldi & Big Picture Media, Sean Lawton & Keppler Speakers, Kevin Lyman, Kate Truscott & everyone at

Warped Tour, Cameron Strang & *Relevant Magazine*, Propaganda, Georgina Smith, Kohl Crecelius, Eric James, Zach Williams, Guy Wasko, Caleb Clardy, Brad Lomenick, Juliet Korver, Kim Kuo, Megalyn Echikunwoke, Micah Smoak, Nathan Thompson, Jess Bowen, Josh Montgomery, Brian Logan Dales, Andy Barron, Joaquin Phoenix, Yael Averbuch, Chloe Grabanski, Keltie Knight, Christina Perri, Stacy Reader, Sophia Bush, Brandi Cyrus, Miley Cyrus, Scott Harrison, Bruce Fitzhugh, Alex Collins, Ryan Anderson, and John Heelan.

i wanted a unique picture of fireworks for the cover. i searched and searched and it turned out a Canadian guy by the name of Andy White had taken the perfect photo. Thanks, Andy, for capturing that moment and for being willing to share it.

Finally, thank you to Joel Fotinos, Sara Carder, Joanna Ng, and Brianna Yamashita at Tarcher Penguin. i actually have no idea what the book proposal process is like, because we took the first offer, because you guys are everything we could have hoped for in a publisher. (The famous cartoon penguin on the back cover is a pretty awesome bonus.) Thanks for your belief in me, and thanks for allowing me to be myself. Thanks especially to Sara, who asked great questions and challenged me to be a better writer.

P.S. The Fray's "Be Still" was on repeat as i wrote much of the new material for this expanded edition.

i hope the new words find their way to m.

TO WRITE LOVE ON HER ARMS.

If you're struggling, please know that it's okay to ask for help. Great help exists and i've met countless people whose lives suggest it's possible to change. No matter what you're facing, reaching out to a counselor, joining a support group, or even calling a hotline can be a great place to start.

The resources listed below are taken from the FIND HELP section of the TWLOHA website. For an extensive list, including local resources (by state, within the USA) as well as international resources, please visit TWLOHA.com. When reaching out to treatment providers, we encourage people to begin by connecting with licensed mental health providers.

HELPLINES

Crisis Text Line offers free, 24/7 support for people in crisis. A trained crisis counselor receives the text and responds quickly. Text TWLOHA to 741-741 | www.crisistextline.org

National Child Abuse Hotline offers crisis intervention, information, and referrals to emergency, social services, and support resources. 1.800.4.A.CHILD (422-4453) | www.childhelp.org/hotline

National Domestic Violence Hotline provides a vital link to safety for women, men, children, and families affected by domestic violence. 1.800.799.SAFE (799-7233) | www.thehotline.org

National Suicide Prevention Lifeline provides free and confidential emotional support to people in suicidal crisis or emotional distress 24 hours a day, 7 days a week. 1.800.273.TALK (273-8255) | www .suicidepreventionlifeline.org

Rape, Abuse & Incest National Network (RAINN) is America's largest anti–sexual assault organization. 1.800.656.HOPE (656-4673) | www.rainn.org

The Trevor Project provides crisis intervention and suicide prevention for LGBTQ youth. 1.866.4.U.TREVOR (488-7386) | www.thetrevorproject.org

Veterans Crisis Line provides confidential help for veterans and their families. 1.800.273.8255 (press 1) | www.veteranscrisisline.net

COUNSELING AND TREATMENT

American Association for Marriage and Family Therapy will assist you in locating a marriage and family therapist in your area. www.therapistlocator.net

American Psychological Association: The APA's Psychologist Locator makes it easy for you to find practicing psychologists in your local area. http://locator.apa.org

Befrienders Worldwide is a dynamic and expanding global network of 349 emotional support centers in thirty-two countries across five continents. www.befrienders.org

Substance Abuse and Mental Health Service Administration: SAMHSA's Substance Abuse Treatment Locator is an online source of information for people seeking treatment facilities for substance abuse/addiction and/or mental health problems. www.findtreatment.samhsa.gov

SUPPORT GROUPS

Adult Children of Alcoholics exists for adults who grew up in alcoholic or dysfunctional homes and who exhibit identifiable traits that reveal past abuse or neglect. www.adultchildren.org

The Al-Anon Family Groups are a fellowship of relatives and friends of alcoholics who share their experience, strength, and hope. www.al-anon.org

Alcoholics Anonymous (AA) is an international fellowship of men and women who have had a drinking problem. Their primary purpose is to help people stay sober and help other alcoholics to achieve sobriety. www.aa.org

In the Rooms offers a free database of anonymous 12-step meetings all over the world, as well as forums where members can connect with other people in recovery. www.intherooms.com

The Nar-Anon Family Groups are for relatives and friends who are concerned about the addiction or drug problem of a loved one. www.nar-anon.org

Narcotics Anonymous (NA) is an international, community-based association of recovering drug addicts with more than 43,900 weekly meetings in more than 127 countries worldwide. www.na.org

ADDITIONAL RESOURCES

Active Minds empowers students to change the conversation about mental health on college campuses. www.activeminds.org

American Foundation for Suicide Prevention (AFSP) exists to understand and prevent suicide through research, education, and advocacy. www.afsp.org

The Jed Foundation exists to promote emotional health and prevent suicide among college and university students. www.thejed foundation.org

The Matthew Shepard Foundation seeks to replace hate with understanding, compassion, and acceptance through educational, outreach, and advocacy programs. www.matthewshepard.org

National Alliance of Mental Illness (**NAMI**) is the nation's largest grassroots mental health organization dedicated to building better lives for the millions of Americans affected by mental illness. www.nami.org

National Eating Disorders Association supports individuals and families affected by eating disorders, and serves as a catalyst for prevention, cures and access to quality care. www.nationaleating disorders.org

Self-injury Outreach and Support (**SiOS**) provides information and resources about self-injury to those who self-injure, those who have recovered, and those who want to help. www.sioutreach.org

USA Cares provides financial and advocacy assistance to post–9/11 active-duty US military service personnel, veterans, and their families. www.usacares.org

CANADA

Canadian Mental Health Association promotes the mental health of all and supports the resilience and recovery of people experiencing mental illness. www.cmha.ca

Canadian Mental Health Crisis Line provides support to individuals experiencing emotional or situational distress, relationship issues, and social isolation. 1.888.353.CARE (353-2273)

Kids Help Phone is Canada's only 24/7 counselling and information service for young people. 1.800.668.6868 | www.kidshelpphone.ca

WE'LL SEE YOU TOMORROW

None of this ends tonight. This was a taste. This was a start. We keep going and we go together. We lean on people and we invite people to lean on us. We ask honest questions and we give honest answers. We ask for help, because we know that it's okay to ask for help.

Above all else, we choose to stay. We choose to fight the darkness and the sadness, to fight the questions and the lies and the myth of all that's missing. There is much not missing. We choose to stay, because we are stories still going. Because there is still some time for things to turn around, time to be surprised and time for change. We stay because no one else can play our part.

Life is worth living. We'll see you tomorrow.

ABOUT THE AUTHOR

Jamie Tworkowski grew up in Melbourne Beach, Florida, where he fell in love with surfing. From an early age, Jamie dreamed of working in the surf industry. In 2002 at the age of twenty-two, Jamie was hired by the clothing brand Hurley, to be their sales rep for the state of Florida. If Hurley hiring Jamie at twenty-two surprised some people, Jamie quitting four years later to start a charity—that surprised them even more.

The charity started with a story. In March 2006, Jamie wrote a piece called *To Write Love on Her Arms,* about his friend Renee Yohe, who was struggling with depression, addiction, self-injury, and thoughts of suicide. Jamie posted the story as a blog on MySpace, and began selling t-shirts as a way to raise money for Renee's treatment. The story quickly went viral and led to To Write Love on Her Arms (TWLOHA) becoming a non-profit organization in 2006.

Supported by bands such as Switchfoot, Anberlin, and Paramore, TWLOHA became widely recognized in the music community, and the organization's message of hope and help began to make its way around the world. The organization now has one of the largest online audiences of any non-profit. The TWLOHA team has responded to more than 200,000 messages from 100 countries. TWLOHA has also donated more than $1.6 million to treatment and recovery.

In 2009, Jamie became the first non-musician to win an MTVU Woodie Award, beating out Alicia Keyes and John Legend to win the Good Woodie Award. In 2011, TWLOHA won the $1,000,000 grand prize at the American Giving Awards. In 2013, the organization used that money to take its flagship event, HEAVY AND LIGHT, to eighteen cities across America. In March 2015, the film *To Write Love on Her Arms* was released by Sony Pictures. Renee Yohe is played by Kat Dennings, and Jamie is played by Chad Michael Murray.

For his work, Jamie has been interviewed by *NBC Nightly News*, *CBS Sunday Morning*, CNN, and *Rolling Stone* magazine. Jamie spends much of his time on the road, telling the TWLOHA story and encouraging audiences at universities, concerts, and music festivals. TWLOHA events have taken Jamie all across America, and as far away as Australia and the United Kingdom.

A proud uncle, Jamie continues to live in Melbourne Beach, Florida. In addition to surfing, he loves basketball and music.

Follow: @JamieTworkowski | @TWLOHA
Questions: E-mail info@twloha.com